Nicole Schwa

De-Centering History Education

Creating Knowledge of Global Entanglements

INTER-AMERICAN STUDIES
Cultures – Societies – History

ESTUDIOS INTERAMERICANOS
Culturas – Sociedades – Historia

Volume 31

Nicole Schwabe

De-Centering History Education

Creating Knowledge
of Global Entanglements

ᴜᴠᴠᴛ Wissenschaftlicher Verlag Trier

Copublished by
UNO University of New Orleans Press

De-Centering History Education:
Creating Knowledge of Global Entanglements /
Nicole Schwabe. Translation by Alexander Kornberg. Editing by Erika Abril. –
(Inter-American Studies | Estudios Interamericanos; 31)
Trier: WVT Wissenschaftlicher Verlag Trier, 2021
    ISBN 978-3-86821-828-2
New Orleans, LA: University of New Orleans Press, 2021
    ISBN 978-1-60801-214-5

SPONSORED BY THE

Federal Ministry
of Education
and Research

The project, on which this book is based, has been funded by the German Federal Ministry of Education and Research (Bundesministerium für Bildung und Forschung, BMBF). The responsibility for the content of this publication lies with the author.

Cover Image: Nicole Schwabe
Cover Design: Brigitta Disseldorf

Library of Congress Cataloging-in-Publication Data
Names: Schwabe, Nicole, author. | Kornberg, Alexander, translator.
Title: De-centering history education : creating knowledge of global
  entanglements / Nicole Schwabe.
Description: Trier : Wissenschaftlicher Verlag Trier ; New Orleans, LA :
  University of New Orleans Press, [2021] | Series: Inter-American studies
  : cultures - societies - history = Estudios interamericanos : cultures -
  sociedades - historia ; volume 31 | Translation by Alexander Kornberg. |
  Includes bibliographical references. | In English, translated from the
  original German.
Identifiers: LCCN 2020044529 | ISBN 9781608012145 (paperback)
Subjects: LCSH: History--Study and teaching--Germany. | Historical
  geography--Study and teaching--Germany. | History--Philosophy. |
  Teaching--Methodology. | Space perception--Germany. |
  America--History--Study and teaching--Germany.
Classification: LCC E16.5 .S39 2021 | DDC 901--dc23
LC record available at https://lccn.loc.gov/2020044529

Publisher: WVT Wissenschaftlicher Verlag Trier, Postfach 4005, D-54230 Trier,
Bergstraße 27, D-54295 Trier, Tel. 0049 651 41503, Fax 41504, www.wvttrier.de, wvt@wvttrier.de

Copublisher: University of New Orleans Press, 2000 Lakeshore Drive, Earl K. Long Library,
Room 221, New Orleans, LA 70148, United States, 504-280-7457, unopress.org

Table of Contents

Preamble

The project 'Knowledge of Global Entanglements' is an attempt to make a contribution to educational practice from the standpoint of science, more precisely from the perspective of interAmerican studies. In order to provide concrete examples of how the findings from theoretical and empirical discussions of the Americas as Space of Entanglements and current discussions from the social and cultural sciences can be conveyed in schools. In the course of reorienting regional studies, the interAmerican perspectives are focusing on transregional dynamics. The approach of investigating the Americas as an interAmerican area of entanglements makes it possible to show cross-border dynamics, processes of deterritorialization and the intertwining of local, national, regional and transregional exchange processes and reference levels (Kaltmeier 2014, 178).

The aim of this theory-practice transfer is not to put our own research emphases additively on the already too full curricula. Rather, the focus is to contrast the production of knowledge in schools with alternative approaches, and to formulate impulses that question the exclusive national narrative, as well as, imparting closed cultural concepts in the classroom. The project focuses on the production of teaching materials for school, whose geographical starting point is – according to the regional focus of our research work – the Americas (from Canada and the USA via Mexico, the Caribbean to Central and South America). Here, phenomena of global significance manifest themselves, such as migration, social inequalities, resource conflicts, the effects of climate change and environmental changes, dealing with ethnic diversity or the presence of colonialism. The series was significantly funded from 2014 to 2019 by the Federal Ministry of Education and Research as a transfer project within the interdisciplinary research project 'The Americas as Space of Entanglements'.

Numerous members of the Center for InterAmerican Studies, including didactic specialists at the University of Bielefeld were very enthusiastic about this project idea, and their commitment is to be thanked for the versatility of the resulting materials. The conceptual development of the teaching units was discussed in interdisciplinary working groups. Tandems from specialist scientists and didactic specialists have proved to be particularly effective in this respect. While some contributed results and ideas from their own research work, others made implementation work possible thanks to their wealth of experience in teaching the subject and, last but not least, their knowledge of the framework conditions of schools. Interdisciplinarity is a fundamental feature of the project. This becomes very clear in the composition of the working group, but also in the materials produced. A central objective of the project was to identify niches, which allow the connection to the parameters of formal education and the use of the materials in school teaching. The task of finding the right balance between familiar topics and new impulses generated by the scientific debate, has continuously accompanied the development of the project.

1. Introductory Remarks

Every production of knowledge is based on the – usually only implicitly visible – understanding of the world. These assumptions shape our perception of the past and our narratives about it. Historiography must, therefore, always be regarded as a situated and context-dependent narrative about the past. Materials for history education also precede the authors' assumptions, which too often remain unreflected. The same applies to curricula whose authors are usually not even made public. A transparent discussion about socially situated premises and worldviews, which are reflected in our narratives of history, is a prerequisite for a democratic negotiation of them. This is not only about the question of what content is taught and learned in schools, but even more significant is a reflection of basic attitudes and perspectives on the world that are inherent to the scholar or what has been learned.

What view on other countries, other regions of the world or other people is taught in history education in Germany? And when we start from Edward Said's thesis, which is fundamental for postcolonial theory, that the construction of the *Other* has a fundamental function for the construction of one's *Own*, this question about the view of the avoidably foreign is accompanied by the question about the avoidably own (Said 2010 [1978]).

When we deal with people or societies in the past, they are all foreign to us first and foremost. We have never met them and will never have the opportunity to do so. Life was different then, than it is now. In order to understand why people at some point in the past acted a certain way and not differently, or to understand what was imaginable at all, a step-by-step and reflected approach is needed. Learning to deal with this difference is a major task of history education. In contrast, however, in a history education oriented towards German national history, the unquestioned notion dominates that we deal with *our* history which is certainly justified, but that could lead to great misunderstandings and false conclusions about the past, as well as the present. As history didacticians and teachers, we must ask ourselves what social self-image is conveyed in the classroom this way. This knowledge production is most likely to become tangible in teaching materials or textbooks. This state-authorized information is considered socially correct and objective; moreover, the knowledge imparted in school is significant. The knowledge conveyed in schools is an expression of a cultural knowledge order and at the same time constructs social order (Müller-Matthis and Wohnig 2017, 5).

The identity-forming function of history means that the teaching of history has a special role to play here. Criticism of the enormous deficits of history teaching in Germany with regard to the imparted knowledge of the world has been around for years. For example, as early as the 1990s Michael Riekenberg and the history didactician Bodo von Borries took a critical look at the knowledge conveyed by textbooks about Latin America and identified massive gaps in knowledge and significant errors in textbooks (Riekenberg and Georg Eckert Institute for International Textbook Research 1990). Even beyond the level of textbook analysis, history didactics has been criticizing curricula frameworks and the structuring of school knowledge production for years. In history education, social, national and cultural events of other countries and regions, as well as transregional entanglements, are often ignored (Völkel 2013; Grewe 2016). This comes from a 19th-century traditional way of thinking. The traditional chronology of "the" history is limited to a Western-European context of tradition from Greek antiquity via the Roman Empire to the "modern world." At the center of this world is the German nation. Therefore, curricula and textbooks have a consistent national internal perspective (Popp 2005, 498-499).

However, if history teaching does not want to lose touch with the present and future challenges, including the students' living worlds, it must face social change and not remain in a historical nostalgia that contributes neither to an understanding of the past nor an orientation to the present. Globally, acting protagonists, transnational exchange relations or the circulation of ideas, goods and people are not new phenomena and a discussion of historical entanglements in the past can make a contribution to globally connected thinking. In times of global crises, it is of fundamental importance to understand the context and to look beyond the national horizon. If there is no place for it in history lessons, the lessons fail at a crucial point. Equally urgent is the examination of the identity-giving function of history in the context of a worrying rise of xenophobic and far-right ideologies and violence. An unreflected national frame of reference, and the lack of discussion of spatial dimensions in history teaching provide a foundation for instrumentalization through far-right ideologies.

To look at the didactics of history from the regional studies viewpoint, offers the possibility to create a certain distance to the subject, but at the same time, there is the danger of overlooking the debates within the discipline and its expertise in historical learning. In order to react to this problem, the following theoretical impulses from *Area Studies*, *Global* and *Entangled History*, will be brought together with the respective points of reference in the historical-didactic debate. This way, these theoretical approaches are to be made tangible for a didactic discussion and give impulses for the *decentering* of history education in Germany. An approach to entangled space that views space, time and social affairs as interwoven dimensions within and among themselves, follows the demands of the US geographer and urban researcher Edward Soja to expand the geographical view. Soja appeals for society, space and time to be thought altogether. He is concerned with a fundamental change of our relation to the world and the acquisition of knowledge about the world (Soja 2008, 252). "We must think the temporal and the spatial, history and geography, together" (Soja 2008, 252).[1]

With his concern to create a spatial awareness, Soja stands in the context of a new spatial conjuncture in the cultural and social sciences. The collective term *Spatial Turn* encompasses a wealth of spatial approaches from various disciplines, that vehemently reject-

---

1   Unless otherwise stated, all translations of citation and titles from German have been made by Alexander Kornberg.

ed the thesis of the *End of Geography (Verschwinden des Raums)* which originated in media theory (Döring and Thielmann 2009, 13-14). This thesis refers to the rapid progress in the field of information and communication technologies since the end of the 20th century. With these revolutionary changes in mind, it was argued that new technological developments such as the Internet or mobile telephony had not only contributed to a shrinking of perceived distances in contemporary perception but had even helped to overcome space.

The critics reacting to this did not doubt the relevance of these events but argued that the material sphere of social life continued to exist and that geography remained a constitutive element of social relations. On the contrary, one is confronted with an expansion of the geographical area through new technologies. Karl Schlögel, for example, emphasizes the emergence of a new social-spatial connection through virtual space, which lies above the existing geographical space (Schlögel 2016 [2003], 36-37).

While the theoretical references are often older, the term *Spatial Turn* itself first appears in Edward Soja's monograph 'Postmodern Geographies' in 1989, according to Döring and Thielmann. In it, Soja criticized the forgetfulness of space in the tradition of historical-materialist historiography, referring to Henri Lefebvre's work and in particular to his book 'La production de l'espace' (Lefebvre 2000 [1974]) published in 1974 (Döring and Thielmann 2009, 7). In addition, the terminology *Spatial Turn* is often traced back to the literary scholar Fredric Jameson. After years of privileging the category of time, he sees the *spatialization of the temporal* as a characteristic feature of postmodernism (Döring and Thielmann 2009, 8). In order to underline this transition, a Foucault quotation from 1967 is often used: "The great obsession of the 19th century, as we know, was history (...). Our time, on the other hand, could be understood more as an age of space" (Foucault, here quoted after Döring and Thielmann 2009, 9).

This remark by Foucault suggests that the preoccupation with spatial theories is actually older, and that central fundamental debates already took place in the 1960s and 70s. Points of reference in this debate are the works of Michel Foucault, Henri Lefebvre and David Harvey (Belina and Michel 2007, 14). Edward Soja also traces the theoretical tradition of *Spatial Turn* back to first advances of Martin Heidegger's and Jean-Paul Sartre's critical philosophy. However, these individual efforts were only bundled much later and contributed to a valorization of the spatial perspective (Soja 2003, 271).

Therefore, the collective term covers a broad spectrum of different approaches. In addition, there are very different understandings of the scope of this spatial research. While for some it is only a rather fast-moving fashionable term, others modestly speak of a change of perspective, while Edward Soja postulates a transdisciplinary paradigm shift (Döring and Thielmann 2009, 13). Even if the interest in the research landscape is currently swinging back, and temporality is being brought more into focus again; it seems wrong and comes from a lack of engagement with the theoretical debates of the field to view the *Spatial Turn* as a passing fashion trend. The impulses rather form a fundamental theoretical basis that can no longer be ignored. Because if we understand the spatial dimension, not as a purely additive dimension, but as fundamentally entangled with the social and the temporal dimension, then these dimensions are also changed if space, time and social things are not thought of separately but conjointly.

In regards to school teaching, the assumption of an urgent paradigm shift and the demand for an equal inclusion of the dimension of space is key. As both – curricula and materials for school teaching – have fundamental deficits in this respect. It is dominated by an unreflected national narrative that persists, despite vehement criticism on the part of historical didactics. The history didactician Bodo von Borries explores questions about a historical-political education that provides students with orientation in dealing with current social challenges and states:

> Do we actually include an extensive teaching unit on a non-European cultural heritage ('other high culture') for its own right (for its own sake) and in its own long-term development into our history

lessons? Or do our students continue to believe – guided and se-
duced by history lessons – that the 10% of Europeans would be
alone in the world or at least far superior in value to all others (just
because 'historical')? (von Borries 2008, 28)

This criticism by Borries – now more than ten years old – can probably be repeated in the same way today, looking at school education. The predicament remains, that the common structuring of the
teaching content of history education in the Federal Republic of
Germany in 2019 is still primarily oriented towards a national narrative and – as Susanne Popp puts it in a nutshell – that learners are
hardly given the opportunity to perceive a *nostrocentric* meaning
structure as such (Popp 2005, 499). Following this criticism of cen-
tering historical learning on an imagined "we-group", I plead for a
de-centering of history education and to overcome the national
identitary reference points.

This goes hand in hand with the demand to strengthen knowledge about non-European societies and their history – previously
marginalized perspectives – in the classroom. However, this is not
about the addition of different national histories, but about a fundamental rethinking and the development of a relational, entangled
history. A *de-centering* of history teaching means to openly discuss
its unquestioned center and discarding the tunnel vision that tempts
one to explain German history only from within itself.

2. Between Theory and Practice

2.1. The Series of Teaching Materials 'Knowledge of Global Entanglements'

I am going to approach the *de-centering* of history education first through a retrospective and look back at the conceptual development of the series of teaching materials 'Knowledge of Global Entanglements'.

Figure 1: Project graphic CIAS teaching material series

The starting point is the project graphic created for public relations purposes, which represents the central theoretical points of reference of the series: A classroom from which we look out into the world. A world marked by global power asymmetries and transregional exchange, as well as, a constant hybridization of cultures. In the background of this fragment of the world, a high-rise complex can be seen, which is a detail of the Frankfurt skyline. However, this sky-scraper might as well be located in Mexico City, Beijing or Singa-pore. Next to it there is a temple pyramid, which is probably also difficult to locate for most. It is the central building of the city of Tikal in the Petén region of northern Guatemala, one of the most important cities of the classical Mayan period. This temple was es-pecially used for ceremonial purposes and was a gateway to the af-terlife (*inframundo*) for the contemporaries. A symbol of power, similar to the buildings of the Frankfurt skyline, with the exception that Frankfurt's bank buildings did not incorporate themselves into the landscape until more than 1000 years later. Today Tikal is no longer a center of power, but a tourist attraction, and the highest building in the European city of Frankfurt belongs to Commerz-bank.

Figure 2: High-rise complex in Frankfurt a. M. (Germany)[2]

---

2   Christian Wolf, Frankfurter Skyline (Blick von der Deutschherrn-brücke, August 2015), URL: https://de.wikipedia.org/wiki/Liste

Figure 3: Temple pyramid of Tikal[3]

With luck, a student in Germany today learns on which continent Guatemala is located. But why have we never really learned anything about the Maya in school, while in Latin America (from Mexico to Patagonia) Western European history is to be found as "universal history" on the curricula? To describe this global asymmetry of knowledge, the Indian historian Dipesh Chakrabarty is used to refer to a cosmopolitanism of the province and a provincialism of the metropolises. Chakrabarty uses everyday observations to describe these inequalities between European and non-European, i.e. non-Western, history. With a view to science, he states that:

> Historians from the Third World feel obliged to take European history into account, whereas historians from Europe, for their part, see no need to reciprocate this interest. (...) 'They' capture their works in relative ignorance of non-Western history, without this apparently

---

_der_Hochh%C3%A4user_in_Frankfurt_am_Main#/media/Datei: Skyline_Frankfurt_am_Main_2015.jpg.

3   Tikalas, URL: https://de.wikipedia.org/wiki/Datei:Tikalas.jpg.

affecting the quality of their work. This, however, is a gesture that 'we' cannot reciprocate. (Chakrabarty 2010, 41)

This correlation is also reflected in teaching at universities. In an introductory sociology lecture at the University of Buenos Aires, it goes without saying that students read Max Weber, Althusser, Foucault or Karl Marx (Universidad de Buenos Aires 2009). It remains unquestioned, not only to what extent social theories – which were developed in completely different historical and social contexts – are suitable for dealing with social questions in the region, but also why nobody in Europe has to be ashamed of not knowing who Julieta Kirkwood or José Carlos Mariátegui were.

This subalternity of non-Western history and knowledge production can also be observed in school education. How do we manage to overlook other parts of the world so consistently? What part does school and especially history education play in this? And what consequences does this behavior have for social self-understanding?

In order to analytically grasp these historically grown knowledge asymmetries and power structures, the Peruvian sociologist Aníbal Quijano speaks of the *coloniality of power* (Quijano 2016, 62). Decolonial theoretical approaches that refer to the work of Quijano counter this colonial matrix of knowledge with alternative forms of knowledge production (Mignolo 2012, 23). They differ from the postcolonial theoretical approaches, more strongly received in the Anglo-American linguistic area, in particular in their context of origin. While postcolonial theory is primarily concerned with colonial expansion since the 19th century, decolonial theorists have a different historical and geographical focus, concentrating on the colonial experience and continuities of 16th century colonialism (Mignolo 2012). The influence of postcolonial and decolonial approaches on the research landscape contributed to the development of a historical and historiographical approach of Entangled History, which turns away from a separatist understanding of space, i.e. the understanding of nationally or regionally closed units, and instead begins to look at the interludes, transcultural circulations and entangled influences, which for a long time received no attention at all (Randeria and Römhild 2013, 17). This is accompanied by a critique of viewing world problems only from a bird's eye perspective, and since the 2000s there have been increasing approaches to link specific local knowledge with global dynamics (CIAS Concept Dossier, 2018).

These local perspectives and changes of outlook, as well as the inclusion of specific knowledge of different protagonists; which are barely perceptible from a bird's eye view, are also reflected in the graph on the project described above. A mass of protesting youths can be identified. The photo was taken at a student protest rally in Santiago de Chile. The voices of these young people who explain exactly why they go out on the street including the voices of other protagonists who are often overheard, have been given a place in our teaching materials.

Figure 4: Demonstration of students in Santiago de Chile (2015)[4]

---

4   Photo: N. Schwabe.

In school lessons, references to non-European societies usually only emerge as an additive comparative perspective. Global Education, which is more firmly anchored in out-of-school education, usually focuses on problem scenarios and thus leads to a rather one-sided knowledge of societies outside Europe. With our series of teaching materials, we aim to tell other stories about the double continent from the Americas and to break stereotypes. For example, inviting to see Latin America, not as a passive continent of crises, violence, banana production and drug trafficking, but as culturally and politically exciting and very heterogeneous societies with their own challenges and their own history.

Existing conflict situations are not ignored, but they should not be the only narrative. The consequences of this reduction of complex situations and heterogeneous societies to a single narrative was summed up by Nigerian writer Chimamanda Ngozi Adichie in her brilliant TED talk 'The Danger of a Single Story' from 2009:

> The single story creates stereotypes, and the problem with stereotypes is not that they are untrue, but that they are incomplete. They make one story become the only story... I've always felt that it is impossible to engage properly with a place or a person without engaging with all of the stories of that place and that person. The consequence of the single story is this: It robs people of dignity. It makes our recognition of our equal humanity difficult. It emphasizes how we are different rather than how we are similar. (Ngozi Adichie 2009)

With an interAmerican series of teaching materials, we try to spark curiosity for all the other narratives beyond well-known stereotypes. The point is to build social proximity and address the interests of young people, while at the same time, maintaining differences and not falling into a cultural relativism.

To create knowledge about global entanglements does not mean to create more remote knowledge *about* others, but decidedly *different* knowledge. This project is initially oriented towards the human geographer Edward Soja's plea for space, time and society to be thought of altogether. This theoretical impulse forms the conceptual basis of the practical project 'Knowledge of Global Entanglements'.

2.2. Thinking Space, Time and the Social Altogether

Our being or being in the world has three basic ontological dimensions for Soja. It is always social, equally spatial and temporal (Soja 2008, 244). Or in other words: Soja is about a theoretical grip of a socially anchored geo-history. Soja grasps his spatial thinking as a trialectic. He, thus, emphasizes that the three levels of spatial thinking (the spatial, the social and the historical) never stand alone, but must always be thought of as equal and interwoven (Soja 2008, 255).

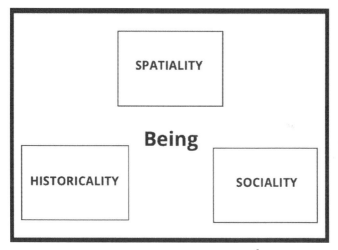

Figure 5: The trialectic of being[5]

Although Soja considers these levels to be of equal importance, he pleads for a strategic privileging of the spatial. For this dimension has been neglected by science for the last two centuries (Soja 2003, 270). With the rise of historiography in the course of the 19th centu-

5   Replica of the figure in Soja 2003, 271.

ry, geography was increasingly pushed back in the academic sphere. For example, the temporal dimension had achieved a dominant position in Germany through the debates on historicism, while geography had been separated from debates on political, social or economic topics. At the same time, disciplines such as economics, political science, ethnology, sociology or psychology developed their subject areas without feeling the need to consider the dimension of space (Soja 2008, 245-46). Jürgen Osterhammel, in his essay 'The Return of Space: Geopolitics, Geohistory and Historical Geography'[6], published in 1998, comes to the conclusion that historicism, through an understanding of history as a development of human will, led in time to a long-lasting suppression of the space category:

> Any idea of a limitation or even determination of the protagonists' actions by nature and the environment – an idea that was still taken for granted in the Enlightenment history – was rejected. A historical science 'beyond historicism' has tacitly adopted this anathema. Even the structures, processes and experiences that it primarily examines are without a location, or at most inscribed in the formal spatial scheme of the nation-state. (Osterhammel 1998, 374)

Hereby Osterhammel draws attention to the consequences of this repression: An unreflected access to space leads to a tacit enforcement of the nation state as the only possible spatial scheme. Karl Schlögel refers to these premises of Soja in his much-quoted work 'In Space We Read Time'[7], first published in 2006, but also pleads for not placing space and time in an antagonistic relationship, for they are rather complementary dimensions (Schlögel 2016, 49).

> Of course, one must not exaggerate the opposition, for on closer inspection it turns out that space and time, comprehended not reductionist and complex, are rather complementary and parallel. Only that in historiographical or sociographical practice more importance

---

6   'Die Wiederkehr des Raumes: Geopolitik, Geohistorie und historische Geographie'.
7   'Im Raume lesen wir die Zeit'.

is given to the time axis. The polemic against a historiography reduced to master narratives must not obscure the view that time,
whether present or past, is no less confusing, chaotic than space.
(Schlögel 2016, 49)

Reinhart Koselleck dedicates a separate chapter to the dimension of
space in his work 'Layers of Time'[8], published in 2000, in which he
states that the old historia, as a general science of experience was
concerned with nature, geography and a chronology. According to
Koselleck, the contrast between historical and scientific categories
of space and time has developed since the 18th century. As a result,
geography has reached a problematic intermediate position (Koselleck 2013 [2000], 79-80). Although Koselleck identifies individual
references to the space category in the works of Johann Gustav
Droysen, Humboldt, Ritter and Ratzel, he notes:

> Faced with the formal alternative of space or time, the overwhelm-
> ing majority of all historians opted for a dominance of time, which
> was theoretically only weakly founded. (Koselleck 2013 [2000], 81)

In German history, Schlögel identified a second incursion that led to
the suppression of space, next to the suppression of geography in
the course of the rise of historicism. Indeed, he notes that the category space was avoided in science after National Socialism. The
category had been used too strongly by the National Socialist ideol-
ogy and was inevitably associated with discussions about Raumnot
(space shortage), Volk ohne Raum (people without space), Lebens-
raum (living space), Ostraum (Eastern space), etc. and therefore
with discussions about the geopolitical, military and economic spatial expansions of National Socialism (Schlögel 2016 [2003], 52).

The resumption of the long discredited spatial debate is consequently a prerequisite for the German context. Until the 1980s, the
debate about space was still regarded as revisionist (Lossau 2012,
185). Even though the suppression of the category is certainly understandable from a historical perspective; it is precisely the lack of

---

8   'Zeitschichten'.

critical discussion that plays into the hands of nationalistic and "völkisch" ideas, especially through the problematic fusion of history, space and cultural identity.

For Soja, this development results in a considerable skewness of the knowledge formation:

> If that is true, then we can assume that much of the accumulated knowledge in our libraries and in our minds, almost everything we have learned, has a deficit in terms of the spatial dimension – since we have not trained for 150 years how to deal with the spatial dimension. (Soja 2008, 247)

Even if it is certainly of advantage, if individual disciplines specialize in a certain perspective and may dominate one of the three dimensions, it makes no sense on the other hand to ignore such a fundamental category and, hence fundamental principles of the constitution of human existence (Soja 2003, 272). In the field of history, the resulting problems for one's own research have been widely discussed in recent years. To translate these discussions into educational practice, we started the series of teaching materials 'Knowledge of Global Entanglements' with a conceptual framework based on the ontological triangle of Space – Society – History demanded by Soja. In a joint brainstorming session of the working group, we assigned central keywords of our own research to this, in order to identify initial starting points for the materials to be produced.

From a spatial perspective, we decided to focus on the Americas as a fluid and multifaceted interwoven space and consequently direct our perception of space beyond nation-state containers. Analogous to our main research areas, the series of teaching materials focuses on globally significant phenomena that illustrate the entanglement of the world in various facets. Phenomena that can only be insufficiently understood if they are not considered as a whole, i.e. along their entire spatial, historical and social extent. The spatial dimension itself is therefore understood as interwoven, but the entanglement of the temporal and social dimensions, as well as the entanglement of the three dimensions is also emphasized.

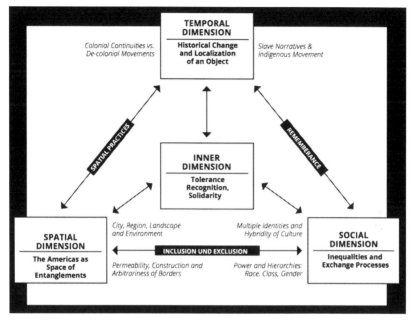

Figure 6: Graphical representation of the conceptual discussion
of the CIAS teaching material series

On this basis, the subject areas of the lecture series will be located
within the temporal dimension and their changes will be examined
in interplay with the socio-political and historical context. We find
such approaches interesting which address the temporality and
memory practices themselves in their multiple layers and temporal
entanglement. Reinhart Koselleck presents a very exciting approach
with the terminological concept of *layers of time* (*Zeitschichten*).
The metaphorical reference to geological terms (*Zeitschichten* and
Sattelzeit are exemplary here) points to a spatial idea of the temporal
dimension at Koselleck. Even though Koselleck does not pursue the
spatial dimension in depth, this pictorial language seems to be a
starting point for an integration of spatial and temporal dimensions.
Koselleck uses time layers to describe superimposed levels of time
of different duration and origin, which nonetheless exist simultane-
ously (Koselleck 2013 [2000], 9). A starting point that is also fun-

damental for an understanding of time understood as *Entangled Temporality*.

In the social dimension, inequalities and exchange processes are emphasized. Thus, on the one hand, asymmetrical power structures and unequal distribution structures along intersectionally interwoven categories such as race, social class and gender. At the same time, the hybridity of culture and multiple dimensions of belonging will be examined in the social dimension. Both dimensions are inconceivable without the dimension of space and are placed, through practices of appropriation of space and social inclusion and exclusion processes, in a structurally heterogeneously conceived space.

The students, as subjects of the learning process, form the center of the graphic. This supplement to Soja's model refers to the model of four-dimensions of Global Education by Graham Pike and David Selby (1999). The key words tolerance, recognition and solidarity come from our initial discussions within the working group and represent an intercultural approach aimed at dialogue and horizontality (Kaltmeier and Corona Berkin 2012).

Looking retrospectively at the interdisciplinary spatial debate of recent years, it is difficult to sum up the content of the debate, despite the attention it has received. This may be due to their versatility, as the spectrum of contributions ranges from rather abstract theoretical to objective and concrete translations.

Following Henry Lefebvre's ideas on espace vécu (lived space), Soja pleads on a theoretical level for spatial thinking that goes beyond existing dualisms of spatial thinking. Soja calls this concept of the spatial constitution of being Thirdspace. Soja contrasts this with Firstspace (in Lefebvre's case, perceived space), the direct immediate spatial experience respectively phenomena that can be cartographically depicted and measured, as well as Secondspace (spatial representations or conceived space), the thinking about and the social construction of space.

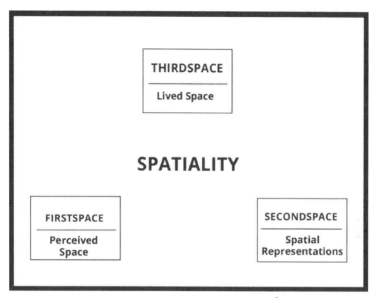

Figure 7: Trialectic of Spatiality[9]

In his well-known work 'La production de l'espace' (1974), Lefebvre juxtaposes a more classical and longtime dominant perspective of geographical analysis with an approach to spatial representation that depicts to him, a much more socially relevant area (Soja 2003, 275 f.).

Concomitant, Lefebvre criticizes the reductionism of large dichotomies. He compares the dichotomy of constructivist and materialist spatial concepts with other dichotomies of western thinking (subject/object; abstract/concrete; action/structure; micro/macro; center/periphery; woman/man). This limitation of view makes it impossible to grasp the actual, lived space. Lefebvre opposed such closed logics and proposed a third way. This can be read as a post-structuralist plea for more flexible forms of thinking that encourages to break out of the constraints of dichotomy and re-conceptualize objects (Soja 2003, 277). In the aftermath, numerous works were based on these theoretical premises.

---

9   Modified replica of the figure in Soja 2003, 274.

The geographer Julia Lossau proposes to assign the contributions to two different dimensions in order to retrospectively analyze the discussions on Spatial Turn. She describes these dimensions of meaning as "symbolic" and "geographical" (Lossau 2012, 186).

She identifies a symbolic semantics especially in poststructuralist approaches, difference-theoretical or power-theoretical perspectives. Space stands for different places or points of view from which meaning is constructed – in context-specific dependence. It is therefore a matter of relational (subject) positions and processes of a production of perception and appropriation that refers to a symbolic level of spatial representation. According to Lossau, this approach can be found particularly in postcolonial works that deconstruct the production of social reality and its spatial order (Lossau 2012, 187): "The central assumption here is that spatial orders are always carried out from a certain perspective or position and that they can therefore only claim partial validity rather than objective validity." (Lossau 2012, 187). Edward Soja points out as well that, for him the most interesting contributions to the expansion of the geographical view and to the Thirdspace come from the cultural sciences. Here, he refers in particular to postcolonial and feminist approaches. For example, the works of Teresa de Lauretis, Rosalyn Deutsche, Barbara Hooper, Gillian Rose, and Gloria Anzaldúa, who investigates the lived space of the Borderlands (Soja 2003, 282-83). He also refers to Edward Said and Homi Bhabha and their central works in postcolonial theory. In his early work 'Orientalism' (1978), Said developed the concept of Imagined Geographies, drawing attention to how the perception of a space is determined by certain imaginaries and discourses. In his works, Homi Bhabha develops a concept that he also calls Thirdspace, referring to a space of openness and hybridity.

Lossau contrasts this in her examination of the debates about Spatial Turn, with approaches that put the figurative meaning of the spatial debate in the center. Hence, these debates focused on a specific region or territory. In regard to globalization debates, it would also be often about the spatial restructuring of world society. Here she notes that despite all efforts to develop transnational social images, a fixation of societies and cultures on spatially limited units continues to dominate (Lossau 2012, 187-88). Lossau also includes debates that deal with bodies and space from a phenomenological perspective and focus consequently on concrete experiences of space (Lossau 2012, 188). She also refers to social-ecological debates and debates on human-natural relations, which are located at the interface between the human and the natural sciences (Lossau 2012, 189).

Reinhart Koselleck's work can also be assigned to this second objective approach. For him, space, as well as time, belongs to the fundamental conditions of history. Space would precede history metahistorically but is itself changed by social and economic factors through which it can be historicized (Koselleck 2013 [2000], 82). Koselleck's reflections, however, remind us of a juxtaposition of what Soja calls Firstspace and Secondspace, meaning the perceived, representational space on one side and the representation and social production of space on the other. A further discussion that would go beyond this dichotomy and would point in the direction of a plea for Thirdspace, cannot be found with Koselleck.

> I would therefore like to understand our questioning of the relation of space and history as bipolar. At one end of the scale is the natural predisposition of every human story. It remains dependent on the specifications of natural conditions or in the narrower sense, to speak with Ratzel, on geographical locations. At the other end of the scale, those spaces emerge which man creates for himself or which he is compelled to create in order to be able to live. (Koselleck 2013 [2000], 83)

The human geographer Julia Lossau considers such spatial semantics, which primarily conceive space as objectively, to be central to an understanding of the world, but criticizes a one-sided focus of these debates on the physical, which equates the return of space with a return of materiality. She refers to and hereby criticizes the prominent work of Karl Schlögel (Lossau 2012, 188-89). In his popular book 'In Space We Read Time'[10] Schlögel sums up the debates about the Spatial Turn for the historiographical debate by postulating:

> There is no story in nowhere. Everything has a beginning and an end. All history has a place. (Schlögel 2016 [2003], 71)

The starting points and exemplary source analyses, which Schlögel identifies in his work, have been met with great approval and interest in history science and in history didactics in particular. However, in human geography, his work has been criticized for focusing on the objective level.

Lossau sees this as a broad Material Turn – subsumed under the figurative-materially understood Spatial Turn – as a reaction to the previous Cultural Turn and the associated focus on language, meaning and texts (Lossau 2012, 189). The reflections presented by Edward Soja underline that we do not do justice to the debates on the Spatial Turn, if we understand them too literal as debates on space as a purely objective category. Rather, for Soja it is about the spatialization of a theoretical building and an understanding of the entanglement of space, time and the social. This interweaving makes Thirdspace a "place of hybridity" that breaks with socially deeply rooted boundaries and confronts them with total openness (Soja 2003, 185-86). An approach of interAmerican entanglement space, as it is understood here, is based on precisely this intertwined and hybrid interspace. By taking off the national tunnel vision and consciously reflecting the dimension of space, completely different phenomena come into view.

---

10 'Im Raume lesen wir die Zeit'.

3. Creating Knowledge of Global Entanglements

3.1. Why Global Education in History Education?

Perspectives from Global and Entangled History in school education not only tie in with current scientific debates, but also provide an answer to current social developments and future challenges. The world is globally interconnected. Hardly anyone would try to deny that today. What is missing, however, is a corresponding global consciousness as well as a basic knowledge of global connections. A large part of the current social challenges can no longer be solved within the national framework. In order to deal with current global crises, climate change, increasing social inequality, the collapse of states and the dramatic rise of violence; in addition to the mass migration movements resulting from all this, cooperation that transcends the borders of nation-state organized societies is indispensable. Zygmunt Bauman comments on this in his essay 'Strangers at Our Door', published in 2016, in response to the media and political panic in the context of massive migration movements:

> Instead of refusing to face the realities of our time, the challenges associated with the dictum 'One planet, one humanity', instead of washing our hands of innocence and ignoring the disturbing differences, inequalities and self-imposed alienation, we must look for ways to come into close and ever-closer contact with others, hopefully leading to a fusion of horizons rather than a consciously induced and self-reinforcing division. (Bauman 2016, 23)

In order to meet its own demands as a social science subject, to teach students the competences "which enable them to understand reality and socially effective structures and processes; and support participation in democratically constituted communities" (Ministerium für Schule und Weiterbildung NRW 2014, 11), history lessons must deal with the complex social present. A history lesson based exclusively on national questions misses this task. This is precisely where the enormous potential of global historical perspectives lies. They can make a fundamental contribution to the development of a global consciousness, a prerequisite for global communication and cooperation.

While historiography in the 19th century was supposed to produce national subjects, Sebastian Conrad considers the promotion of a cosmopolitan self-image to be the central task of the discipline today. For a global perspective is the prerequisite for understanding current conflict situations, from working conditions and the economy, to environmental and climate issues (Conrad 2013, 26). The plea of the history didactician Susanne Popp for a history lesson with a perspective on global history can be connected to precisely this argumentation. That's how Popp writes:

> The world in which adolescents live and the historical culture that surrounds them form (...) central points of reference for the discipline. And today's generation of students is certainly no longer the first, of which can be said, that it can connect with people around the globe, or is used to look at the planet it inhabits with others from an outside perspective, more than any generation before – at least potentially. (Popp 2005, 492)

So, has the youth long since overtaken their parents' and grandparents' generation in terms of global consciousness? According to a study by the Federal Ministry for the Environment, Nature Conservation and Nuclear Safety (BMU) in 2018, for young people in Germany networking via the Internet is just as much a part of their everyday lives as a globalized world in which different regions of the world are easily accessible and where all developments feel somehow connected. They also belong to a generation that has grown up in the context of consecutive crisis scenarios, according to the BMU.

> The euro, financial and debt crisis, the environmental and climate crisis, the global drifting apart of rich and poor, the dismantling of social security systems and increasing precarious employment, the demographic and pension crisis, the challenges posed by migration and the growing threat of terrorism – to name but a few. Some experts call this 'growing up in economic crisis mode'. (BMU 2018, 12)

Of course, young people in Germany cannot be represented as a homogeneous group, but rather have a variety of life situations and the most varied values and ideas of the social situation associated with them, as the SINUS study shows, which is based on milieu research (Calmbach, Borgstedt, Borchard, Thomas and Flaig 2016). But even if not all of them participate equally, young people in Germany grow up in an economically stable situation. This explains why, despite global crisis scenarios, they are looking positively into the future. At the same time, the young people surveyed in the BMU study show an awareness of social inequalities, and for the vast majority cultural diversity is the normal state of affairs. They state that acceptance and respect for other lifestyles is a matter of fact for them (BMU 2018, 12-16).

Compared to previous generations, mobility, travelling abroad and migration are part of everyday life for young people in Germany. The fact that this generation thinks much more globally than adults can even imagine, is demonstrated not only by the school protests Fridays for Future, which call on politicians to act against climate change. The extent to which xenophobic attitudes and right-wing populist ideas also spread among young people; caused by an increasing feeling of insecurity in the context of global crises, as it can be seen from the overall population, cannot be determined from the present youth studies. Against this background, however, a generally optimistic view of the global consciousness of young people should certainly be critically examined. Beyond different attitudes and different life situations, young people today (and not only in Germany) face the common challenge of understanding the current complexity of the world, which is a central prerequisite for participation. Either as voters in the decision of directional questions or through other forms of involvement in politics. From this, it can be concluded that the objective interests of students (in which I include the ability to participate in society and political maturity) here coincide with one's own subjective interests and one's own world.

The project of introducing young people to the debate on global issues can be tied to their interests and derived from their own every

day lives. Global entanglements can be found in the local, in our immediate environment, our own local action is global. Promoting networked thinking that raises awareness of global connections must
become a central task of schools. German sociologist Stephan Lessenich argues in his contemporary analysis 'Next to Us the De-
ludge'[11] (2016) for such a relational perspective on the social world:

> We live in a world of relationships, in both small and large terms.
> We have many relationships with others, sometimes closer, some-
> times more distant. How we live and what we are is determined by
> these social relationships and is unthinkable without them. What we
> do always has an impact on others – just like what we do not do;
> sometimes these are more direct effects, sometimes only indirect,
> sometimes hardly comprehensible. (Lessenich 2016, 48)

Starting from this perspective of entanglement of the social and the
spatial, Lessenich underlines the necessity of an analysis of social
inequalities that goes beyond the nation-state inner perspective
(Lessenich 2016, 53). Lessenich takes structural global power asymmetries into account and comes to the conclusion that certain social
collectives have the chance "to pass on the costs of their own life-
style to others" (Lessenich 2016, 62). In order to get to the bottom
of this process, he focuses his sociological investigation on the Global North, drawing on the concept of Pierre Bourdieu's habitus,
originally developed for intra-societal analysis.

> In this context, the societies of the global North as a whole, despite
> their manifold social-structural inner differentiations, occupy the
> particularly privileged positions. And in relation to these positions
> one can speak of an externalization habitus, of a habitually carried
> out practice by individuals as well as by collectives – status groups
> and social milieus, national communities and ultimately entire re-
> gions of the world – of outsourcing the costs of their way of life to
> third parties and, at the same time, suppressing precisely this struc-
> tural connection from their everyday way of life. (Lessenich 2016,
> 61-62)

---

11   'Neben uns die Sintflut'.

If we transfer Lessenich's analysis to the debate on the orientation of history teaching in Germany initiated here, we should also ask ourselves whether the nation-centered perspective in history education – and in the larger sense the blending out of non-European societies or the global South in school education – is not at all a coincidental remnant of earlier times, but rather a function in a process of legitimizing global social inequalities. Because if we begin to detach ourselves from the inner perspective, this will question the ground on which we stand, the prosperity in this country and our social self-image. Such a broadening of perspective is certainly not painless, and yet we cannot avoid it, if the sociological analyses of the present should be proved right. Thus, Lessenich emphasizes that "the collective psychological trick of the externalization society – 'out of sight, out of mind'" does not work forever and much indicates that soon, not only others but also ourselves will be confronted with the consequences of our life and economy (Lessenich 2016, 75).

In political education, as well as in educational science – since the 1990s, in the wake of the rise of the globalization debate and the upheavals of 1989/90 – the concept of *Global Education* has been associated with the demand that education should respond to global social challenges. The thoughts of this essay can be connected to this. The debate on Global Education is linked to a normative appeal to overcome global social inequalities. Therefore, the educationalists Annette Scheunpflug and Barbara Asbrand understand Global Education as follows:

> Global Learning/Global Education today sees itself as a 'pedagogical reaction to the developmental fact of world society' under the normative perspective of overcoming inequality or oriented towards the model of global justice. (Asbrand und Scheunpflug 2014, 401)

In the context of the United Nations Sustainable Development Goals (SDGs), corresponding efforts in the formal and extracurricular education sector in Germany have been financially supported and promoted on behalf of politics in recent years. Since the mid-2000s, the political agenda for Global Education / Education for Sustainable

Development has been strongly criticized by postcolonial-oriented civic groups. In 2013, the Berlin association glokal published an analysis of educational materials on development policy entitled 'Education for Sustainable Inequality'[12]. In it, the group concludes that the materials analyzed have an overall Eurocentric perspective. Even though there are certainly exceptions, I want to agree with the criticism at this point. Much of the effort to implement Global Education fails to really leave the inner perspective of the externalization society. Instead, the concept of developmental thinking and an understanding of European modernity is retained as an independent process. The preconditions of this success story, the colonial and imperial exploitation and the underdevelopment of other parts of the world are covered up. The internationally renowned German sociologist Maria Mies insists not to succumb to the illusion of being able to solve the problems of the underdeveloped regions of the world through a process of catching-up development modeled on Europe or through development "aid." To draw attention to the connection between global social inequalities and power asymmetries, she proposes the use of the term pair "overdevelopment – underdevelopment." An order that can only be maintained to a limited extent due to the finite nature of vital resources (Mies 2015, 87). However, a corresponding awareness of global interrelationships is hardly developed. The specific contribution that history education can make to this will be discussed below.

In the second edition of the 'Curriculum Framework: Education for Sustainable Development' (KMK, BMZ, and EG 2016), commissioned by the KMK (Standing Conference of the Ministers of Education and Cultural Affairs) and the BMZ (German Federal Ministry of Economic Cooperation and Development) and published by Engagement Global, a chapter on history education was also produced. The inclusion of the school subject in the publication is a central step in the development of the learning field. The introduction to the chapter by Elisabeth Erdmann, Bärbel Kuhn, Susanne

---

12   'Bildung für Nachhaltige Ungleichheit' .

Popp and Regina Ultze refers to the specific contribution of historical learning to the debate on Global Education / Education for Sustainable Development.

> History as a school subject is closely connected to other human, social and cultural sciences. It opens up the historical dimension of past, present and future phenomena in Global Development Education/ESD, which is indispensable for their understanding. (KMK, BMZ, and EG 2016, 240)

In addition, there are other interesting points for the development of approaches to Global Education in history education: the confrontation with continuity and change, multi-perspectivity and the experience of alterity in a historical context are central aspects of historical learning. In order to fully use this potential, well-founded contributions are needed to make approaches to a global perspective of history education tangible, and which translate the scientific debate on approaches of Global History for teaching practice. The present text is also intended to contribute to this.

3.2. Boom of Global History

Just as in general education and political education since the 1990s and increasingly in the 2000s, different protagonists have been dealing with the current developments of a globalized world, in history science too, a reorientation has been taking place since the end of the Cold War and the accompanying geopolitical upheaval. This is where the rise of Global and Entangled History can be seen. While in the USA the rise of global historical perspectives, which stand out from older teleological and Eurocentric universal historical approaches, was already becoming apparent at the beginning of the 1990s, these discussions took place years later in Germany. Initially, the interest in the course of reunification is directed towards a national historiography. It was only in the 2000s, with the rise of the globalization debate, that global and entanglement historical perspectives gained more and more attention in the German debate. For the historian Matthias Middell, the interest in Global History is a reaction to the lack of history in the globalization debate and represents an attempt to oppose it. An actually observable entanglement of the world is shown using the example of the multifaceted interactions of historical protagonists (Middell 2009, 107-108). The historian Karl Schlögel also justifies his interest in space and history with the

> radical changes of space and time in the 20th century, the force of the globalization process and the accelerated implementation of new technologies, the concomitant production of synchronicity and asynchronicity in the narrowest space. (Schlögel 2016, 42)

Similarly, Shalini Randeria and Sebastian Conrad, in their introduction to the much-quoted anthology 'Beyond Eurocentrism'[13], name the debate on globalization as an impulse for the development of new perspectives on Europe's imperial past. This goes hand in hand with the basic assumption that the current world order and thus also current globalization processes are structured by precisely this imperial history (Conrad and Randeria 2013, 32). Their aim is to take a look from a postcolonial perspective at the entanglement of the European and non-European world, which is increasingly attracting attention as a result of the globalization debate, and to make it the starting point for one's own historiography (Conrad and Randeria 2013, 33).

In recent years, a whole series of works have emerged in the field of global historical research that make global entanglements, exchange processes and interdependencies empirically tangible. The fact that the perception of such processes increases rapidly after 1989 does not mean, however, that previously there was no relevant circulation of ideas, goods or people in the world. Global historical approaches in historiography make such entanglements tangible in the past and form a basis for understanding a globally networked world today. A historically founded examination of a connected world makes it possible to counteract the above-mentioned "lack of history in the globalization debate" (Middell 2009, 107), i.e. an incomplete, narrowed perspective on globalization, and to finally under-

---

13   'Jenseits des Eurozentrismus'.

stand its origins. This could be an elementary contribution to the understanding of a contemporary global world. In particular, the fact that the entanglement is concretized in empirical examples, allows a real approach to the nebulous and hardly tangible global.

It is key though, to not restrict the focus of global perspectives in schools to crisis scenarios. Beyond real problems, disintegrating states, progressive climate change and increasing social inequalities, school education must also focus on other topics. Rather, attention should be paid to show as many different global historical approaches in school as possible. The pure focus on problem scenarios, when it comes to non-European societies at school, harbors the dangers of a one-sided, stereotypical narrative (Ngozi Adichie 2009). In addition, the aim is not to entrust students with the task of solving global crises, but rather to prepare them to orient themselves in complex world contexts. At this point, a global perspective should not be confused with the idea of looking at and solving world problems from a "godlike" macro-perspective. Such an understanding of a global consciousness leads in the wrong direction. Instead of omnipotence, Global Education should focus on sensitivity to difference and diversity and, in particular, to one's own location and limitations of perspective.

3.3. Historical Awareness of Space

However, if we go one step further and ask for the implementation of the above-mentioned demand, the conscious reflection of the category of space in history education and the orientation on global historical perspectives in school education, we face the challenge that we hardly know anything about the spatial awareness of students[14]. There are hardly any deeper debates and reliable empirical

---

14   In general pedagogy, the works of Karlheinz Benke 'Geographien der Kinder' ('Geographies of Children') (2005) and Daniela Schmeinck 'Wie Kinder die Welt sehen. Eine empirische Ländervergleichsstudie zur räumlichen Vorstellung von Grundschulkindern' ('How Children Look at the World. An Empirical Country Comparison

research resources that bring together the spatial consciousness of students with the question of historical consciousness. We also lack the categories to talk about the corresponding imaginary worlds and experiential spaces. Hereafter I will talk about personal and social historical spaces of students. Whereby there is no fully developed concept behind it. Consequently, a fundamental discussion has yet to take place, particularly with regard to the linking of the spatial dimension with a temporal dimension and historical consciousness. The personal, direct, concrete experience of space, in my under-standing, is in a reciprocal relationship with an indirect (perhaps symbolic or imaginary) experience of space through narratives about space and the representation of it, e.g. in maps, literature, everyday objects or cultural production. This already leads to the conclusion that individually different, personal spaces understood in this way, are always in an interrelationship with social spaces.

Vadim Oswalt builds a bridge to history education and contrib-utes to further theory development. For Oswalt, the dimension of space and spatial awareness is a prerequisite for historical learning, and he pleads for a deeper examination of this category, which – al-so in didactics of history – has long been neglected. This demand becomes clear in the concise title of his essay 'The Where to What and When'[15] (Oswalt 2010, 233). The debate of spatial awareness within didactics is a fundamental matter to him:

> A space-conscious approach to historical learning should play a role at all levels of curriculum design, in the diagnosis of students' learn-ing requirements and in the embedding and linking of different his-torical methodological points of reference in historical learning. (Oswalt 2010, 233)

Following the findings of various scientific disciplines on spatial perception, Oswalt highlights three exemplary characteristics of

---

Study on the Spatial Perception of Primary School Children') (2007) form interesting connection points.

15   'Das Wo zum Was und Wann'.

spatial perception, which he associates with questions of historical consciousness. These starting points appear central when it comes to anchoring the debate about space in the didactics of history. His comments on this correspond with Edward Soja's trialectic under-standing of space, as Oswalt places the dimension of space in an equal relationship to the dimensions of time and the social in histor-ical learning.

Firstly, Oswalt conceives the experience of space as an individ-ual construct. This understanding is preceded by the assumption that as many spaces as space experiences exist. Oswalt assumes that the personal, selective perception of space and the meaningful linking of spatial experience with meaningful content form a basis for re-memberance. Oswalt transfers these basic assumptions about an in-dividual construction process of memory to collective memory (Os-walt 2010, 224):

> This context of meaning transforms the imagination of space into 'anchors' of memory. The Where usually brings back the Who or What. This happens both in individual and collective memory, in which certain spatial constructs such as region, nation, Europe etc. are linked to a certain collective memory. (Oswalt 2010, 224)

As results of recent brain research show, there is no separate area in the brain for spatial perception, but rather it is part of a neuronal network that connects different sensory perceptions with each other. Through this mixing of sensory, auditory or olfactory perceptions with the imagination and perception of spaces, Oswalt comes to the second conclusion about spatial experience: spatial experience con-cerns different levels of sensory perception and is, therefore, emo-tionally extremely charged. In this way, spaces can also be connected with narratives, which raises the unresolved question of how space and historical narration relate to each other (Oswalt 2010, 224). Oswalt sees the third characteristic of spatial perception as "identi-ty-constitutive" emphasizing that spatial perceptions also fundamen-tally structure the perception of the social and shape the self-con-ception of individuals (Oswalt 2010, 224).

Just as the Here is the starting point of all orientation, the demarca-
tion of the Here from There, of the We from the Other, is key to the
formation of identities that therefore form in spaces. (Oswalt 2010,
224)

Such self-conceptions anchored in space are exploited for political
purposes. Distinctions are given a specific function and are rede-
fined into objective facts. And if we understand Oswalt's spatial experience as a multisensory process that affects different levels of
sensory perception (Oswalt 2010, 225), we can explain the associated emotional charge that can be observed in political discussions
about borders, territorial claims, national and ethnic identities, as
well as migration.

Turning away from the category of space, especially after its
exploitation by the National Socialists, is understandable against
this background, but does not solve the corresponding problem. It
rather makes this unreflected field of historical-political judgment
making really dangerous. It cannot be overemphasized that such a
confrontation represents a central task of historical-political education in times of a global shift to the right and populist politics, both
online and offline.[16]

3.4. Alterity Experience in Historical Learning

In addition to conscious reflection and an extension of the spatial
perspective with regard to the structuring of learning content, which
will be explored in more detail later on, it needs to be referred to the
specific potential of history education in dealing with alterity. In the
context of increasing xenophobia and racism, as well as chauvinis-

---

16 In political education, the matter of emotions in the context of social
    transformations and new discussions about identities and affiliations
    is attributed a key role, as the 14th Federal Congress on Political
    Education on Emotions in Politics and Society (14. Bundeskongress
    Politische Bildung zu Emotionen in Politik und Gesellschaft) (Ger-
    many, 2019) shows.

tic-nationalist positions, a reflected examination of alterity experiences is key. When we deal with the past in history education, we always deal with something foreign. This examination of other ways of thinking and imaginary worlds in the past offers the possibility of questioning one's own or the things that seem natural to us. This gives us the opportunity to change our own positions and develop new perspectives, but also to consolidate our own ideas and justify them more clearly. Reflecting about alterity in history education, Michael Sauer underlines that:

> The prerequisite for understanding others is actually opening oneself up to this historical Other, testing situations and behaviors for oneself in thought, experimenting with the perspectives of the stranger (Sauer 2012, 76).

But this is by no means an easy process and the experiences from history didactics make it clear that students classically tend to apply their own evaluation standards to the past; and thus come to a hasty and rather unhistorical judgment about it. Working towards that, students begin to engage with different ways of thinking and a different social context is a challenge for historical learning (Sauer 2012, 76). A further level of experience of alterity in historical learning can be achieved, if on a meta-level alterity experiences of the past are thematized and the students themselves deal with the encounter, the mutual exchange and interaction of different societies and hybridity of culture becomes concretely tangible in historical examples. Important competences for orientation in the present can be drawn from these historical-cultural experiences of strangeness. If it were possible to leave a national inner perspective in history education, to take other societies in their independent development seriously and to look at one's own history from a different perspective, this would be a central step towards the *de-centering* of historical learning.

4. Learning about Ourselves

4.1. The National Tunnel Vision in History Education

If the demand for a *de-centering* of history education is to actually be applied in schools, we cannot avoid a serious examination of the limits and possibilities of the framework conditions of schools. In this sense, the discussion of curricula is essential. Even though, discussions on the restructuring of history curricula with a view to the topic under discussion are certainly lacking, the following section will start with the existing curricula and will explore how global perspectives can be integrated here.

Classically, history education in Germany begins with prehistory, then jumps to the origins of western culture in the Mediterranean region and comes via the Carolingian Empire to the Christian Middle Ages before German national history begins. In this way – as history didactician Susanne Popp notes – German national history is placed in a tradition representing 5000 years. In addition, Popp identifies numerous references to European history in history education, with reference to the early modern period and modernity, that are not classically national historical. For example, the Cold War and the formation of Blocs in the second half of the 20th century are classical subjects in the classroom. Curricula and textbooks also contain highlight-like exemplary digressions on topics of non-European history (Popp 2005, 498). In addition, maps in textbooks transport worldviews.[17]

Even if not all of the topics of history education are classically national historical, and the criticism that history education provides

---

17 The use of maps in history education is a central topic of the question discussed here. Since we will not go further into this, I would at least like to draw attention to Vadim Oswalt's publication 'Karten als Quelle und Darstellung: Historische Karten und Geschichtskarten im Unterricht' ('Maps as Source and Representation: Historical Maps and History Maps in Teaching'), published 2019 by Wochenschauverlag.

a national tunnel vision seems to quickly falter, the hypothesis remains valid on closer examination.

Susanne Popp concretizes the critique of traditional chronology in history education by speaking of a *nation-centered* narrative.

> Nevertheless, it makes sense to speak of a nation-centered narrative in relation to the German core curriculum. As it describes in short the hardly disputable fact, that the German core curriculum is anchored in the national historical identity and historical culture and that, according to the general social consensus, it also should be. (Popp 2005, 298-99)

For Popp, this *nation-centered* or even *nostro-centric* narrative expresses itself particularly in a consistent inner perspective in teaching materials and curricula; and also in the fact that the relevance of a topic for "one's own" history is a consistent selection criterion. The linchpin of history education is thus "Western European" and especially "German" history (Popp 2005, 499).

Bernd-Stefan Grewe sees the orientation towards the national narrative founded in the history of origin of the subject. Like historiography, history education as a school subject fulfilled the function of legitimizing the nation state as a new political unit from the 19th century onwards. To this end, the discipline was promoted accordingly and Grewe still sees it anchored in this line of continuity today, even though it has been extended by (Western) European points of reference in the meantime (Grewe 2016, 301).

Michael Sauer also comes to the conclusion that in the traditional chronology of history education a canon is handed down that is neither fundamentally discussed nor justified (Sauer 2012, 48). He also draws attention to the fact that, in history didactics, other models for structuring curricula have to be discussed. History education as a school subject is not only confronted with the problem that new content is added over time, but also with the challenge that new research approaches in history science bring along new content and approaches for teaching (Sauer 2012, 42).

A chronological orientation can certainly be justified by the fact that the past becomes only understandable in the context of its past history and the processuality of history can only be made tangible by chronology. But Sauer also points out the problems of such a structuring and so, world-historical considerations are left behind. Additionally, the rigid chronology already structures so clearly, that adaptation to the learning group is severely limited (Sauer 2012, 48-49).

4.2. Consequences of a *Nostrocentric* Historical Consciousness

From the background of the conceptual foundation of a *Trialectic of Being*, thinking of space, time and the social together as presented at the beginning, a structuring of teaching based exclusively on the temporal dimension is clearly deficient. Just as the social dimension certainly cannot be adequately explored if we insist on a traditional personal and event history and renounce perspectives of social, gender or cultural history in the classroom, it is long overdue that global historical approaches arrive in the classroom.

Because an unreflected approach to the dimension of space leads to a fundamental part of the historical learning process to remain hidden, as the historical didactic Vadim Oswalt makes clear with his work. In the classroom, certain spaces are declared important in certain historical phases (without discussing and reflecting on this), others are faded out. This choice of space structures historical learning, but the implications of this specific connection between space and time remain obscure (Oswalt 2010, 226). Empirical work on the consequences of this specific choice of space for historical learning has so far been lacking. For Oswalt, it is due to a cultural tradition, which spaces are considered relevant in which historical phase. There is no open and reflected discussion about the imparted spatial or identitary points of reference.

If we were to seriously consider the question of space selection, the result would certainly not be to abolish national history in teaching. On the contrary, within a nation-state organized society there must also be a discussion in history education about the prerequisites and the origin, as well as the future of this social organizational unit. Hopefully, however, we would succeed in overcoming a *nation-centered, nostro-centric* way of thinking in history education. Only then, students could be empowered to place local and national phenomena in a wider context and be able to comprehend contexts.

National history is not problematic in itself. It becomes critical, however, when the nation state is understood as a hermetic, closed unit and a historical-political consciousness refers exclusively to the national point of reference. Imparting a closed understanding of culture is a logical next step. In a *nation-centered* history education, there is also the danger, not to be underestimated, of the biologization of history and the associated essentialization of culture. History didactician Bärbel Völkel points out, that at the beginning of history education, students are classically introduced to the history of the nation through their own family history. The image of the family tree with its roots, its own ancestors, becomes a metaphor for the didactic imparting of the phenomenon of history. But false conclusions are obvious, if a culturally produced community with a family concept based on biological descent is taught (Völkel 2016, 60-63).

Bärbel Völkel deals with the consequences of such a way of imparting history in her essay 'About the Unwanted Side-Effects of a Traditional Chronological History Education'[18] (Völkel 2013). With reference to the debate about Thilo Sarrazin's polemic book 'Germany Abolishes Itself'[19] and the accompanying discussion on the "German leading culture", which has been continued in recent years by new rights and well-known conservative politicians, she puts forward the thesis that the traditional chronology from antiquity to the present, imparted in history education, bears a co-responsibility for the emotionality of the debate about Islam in Germany (Völkel 2013, 402). For her, the question behind this is:

---

18 'Von ungewollten Nebenwirkungen eines traditionellen chronologischen Geschichtsunterrichts'.

19 'Deutschland schafft sich ab'.

> Should the German nation state in the future be further and further developed into a state nation, with the danger of – for the benefit of compromises owed to the heterogeneity of society – giving up more and more its 'own', the specifically 'German', in the spirit of a common rapprochement and change? Or should the nation be able and allowed to continue to see itself primarily as a cultural nation, in which the 'own' is to be protected against the 'foreign' by a restrictive policy? (Völkel 2013, 402-3)

In this Völkel sees a pending discussion on the formation of historical meaning, duration and change, which falls within the competence of historical didactics, and deals with the consequences of a national narrative, which serves to construct a coherent independent history from antiquity to the present. The idea of a community of descent and values as well as the requirements of solidarity with it, are unintentionally conveyed and historically founded (Völkel 2013, 406-9). Völkel describes this logic as ethnocentric. In this case, ethnocentrism is defined as

> cultural strategy in which the collective identity of one's own group is gained by distinguishing it from other groups in a way that substantially distinguishes one's own social space as a common and familiar space from the social space of others. (Völkel 2013, 409)

Other historiographical approaches become special cases in this logic and that, although the Mediterranean region is treated in antiquity, a look at the early advanced civilizations (e.g. the Aztecs, Maya or Incas) in the Americas at the time of the Middle Ages seems insane, requires no justification at all.

In the structure of the curriculum, the interests or life situations of students – in addition to the challenges they have to deal with today and in the future – are put behind the primacy of national history. Between rigid chronology and cross-school comparative final examinations, teachers have little opportunity to adapt their lessons to the learning group.

The didactics of history strongly criticizes the narratives and the unreflected spatial focus that dominate history education in the Federal Republic of Germany. Thus, the history didactician Bernd-Stefan Grewe considers these scientifically intolerable. He pleads for a history education that is oriented towards global history and that is oriented towards current challenges. Grewe argues that the focus on Western and Central Europe excludes central parts of European history. For example, the role of the Ottoman Empire for the European balance of powers would be forgotten (Grewe 2016, 299-300).

Susanne Popp also sees great potential in the inclusion of global historical perspectives. By comparing German curricula with more globally conceptualized US-American *world history curricula,* she works out fundamental deficits in German history education with regard to a global orientation of historical awareness and historical learning in general. Popp criticizes the fact that in the German *nation-centered* curricula, the abstract reference value of humanity as a historical conceptual parameter is not taken into account. In addition, the students would not be given the opportunity to recognize the given and strongly limited *nostrocentric* perspective as such. The own location dependency and the underlying identity concept are not made transparent (Popp 2005, 499).

> Experience has shown that quite large problems of understanding arise from the nation-centered internal perspective for learners where transnationally significant phenomena, such as industrialization or nation building, are portrayed completely uncommented exclusively in their specific national-historical form and solely in relation to their significance for 'our' history. Then students are usually unable to distinguish between a general and a nostrocentric layer of meaning. (Popp 2005, 501)

She does not see the problem mainly in the location dependency of the narrative in itself. Rather, she assumes that every story is generally centered and not free of references to identity. Moreover, she is concerned with making this limited perspective visible through the inclusion of world and global historical perspectives, which only make it possible to identify other perspectives as nation-centered (Popp 2005, 499). Following this thought, Teresa Gärtner underlines the consequences of this lack of classification in a larger context:

> Without a permanently present world scale, this leads to a potential uniqueness of one's own location, whereby the specific cannot be separated from the alleged general. This national historical narrative constructs a 'non-us' group with oppositional characteristics to the 'we' group to emphasize its identity. (Gärtner 2012, 36)

In order to avoid this, she calls for the history of the "non-us" group not to be further marginalized in history education, but to be thematized decisively and to make experiences of alterity and changes in perspective a fundamental component of historical learning (Gärtner 2012, 36).

Global history perspectives in history education can, therefore, not be reduced to a reflection on the territorial points of reference, for geographies are interwoven with certain imaginary worlds, historical narratives and identity formation. The perception of the past is determined by our position in the world, is accompanied by different sensory perceptions and cognitive maps, as well as spatial stereotypes solidified therein (Oswalt 2010, 225). Historical learning, hence, urgently needs to be perceived in its spatial dimension, and spatial references in history teaching need to be clearly justified.

5. Impulses for the De-Centering of History Education

Building on the criticism of the lack of reflection on spatial references in history teaching presented in the previous chapter, a practical approach to implementing the demand for a *de-centering* of history education will be developed below. For this purpose, reference
is made to the theoretical impulses of *Entangled History*, which refers to the premises of the *Spatial Turn*.

Since the 1970s, critical trends have prevailed in history science, rejecting all-encompassing master narratives. These advances
can be understood as an attempt to open up historical science and to
create space for protagonists who previously had no place in history
(Middell 2009, 104). Social and cultural history approaches, everyday history, oral history or approaches to gender history have not
only opened up new perspectives but have also looked at completely
new social spaces. Post- and decolonial approaches, which were
driven primarily by intellectuals from the Global South, argued in
favor of breaking away from Western development narratives and
incorporating local, subaltern perspectives into their own research
(Kaltmeier 2012, 25). Thus, epistemic foundations of knowledge
production as well as political, social, economic and cultural power
asymmetries of a postcolonial world order are examined. *Entangled
History* follows these developments and discussions and also looks
at the interconnection of societies from a transcultural perspective.
This means a renunciation from nations, civilizations and closed
units as analysis categories. Rather, they are regarded as products of
global exchange processes and not as natural units and factual investigation spaces (Bauck and Maier 2015).

By criticizing exclusively national narratives in historiography,
the approach overlaps extensively with recent debates in *Global
History* and can consequently be seen as part of a new debate within
it. The approach, however, clearly distinguishes itself from older
world history as well as authors of *Global History*, who presume a
closed understanding of culture or Western superiority in their
works (Bauck and Maier 2015). In contrast to universal history,

modern global historical approaches do not pursue the goal of developing comprehensive historical regularities. Moreover, *Global History* cannot be equated with a global, all-encompassing macro-perspective. Recent works in *Global History* often start locally and make global exchange processes and local entanglements empirically tangible (Grewe 2016, 302).

In contrast to the 20th century, when the preoccupation with world history was rather parallel to the other approaches of historiography and fell within the remit of older historians, numerous empirical studies by increasingly younger scientists have been produced in recent years. In addition, very different approaches of history science are oriented towards global historical perspectives. From economic history and environmental history to more social- or cultural-historical works, global historical approaches are naturally included (Conrad 2013, 13).

Hereafter, central reflections on *Global* and *Entangled History* are presented and associated with the corresponding discussions within history didactics. In history didactics, a corresponding debate about global historical perspectives within education can be observed. Here, for example, one can refer to the anthology 'Curriculum World History. Interdisciplinary Approaches to Globally Oriented History Education'[20] (2008) by Susanne Popp and Johanna Forster.

5.1. Turning Away from Methodological Nationalism

Global historical approaches argue for overcoming a *methodological nationalism*[21]. This criticism refers not only to the focus on events within the nation-state, but also to methodological approaches derived from the perspective of the nation-state. Often there is also reference to *container thinking* and criticism that thinking of nation

---

20 'Curriculum Weltgeschichte. Interdisziplinäre Zugänge zu einem global orientierten Geschichtsunterricht'

21 The term was coined by the German sociologist Ulrich Beck.

states as closed spatial containers can lose sight of social contexts and exchange relations beyond these established units (Conrad 2013, 24). With reference to history education, the criticism of a *nation-centered* curriculum presented in the previous chapter can be cited. But methodological nationalism can also have an effect at other levels, e.g. through the inadequately reflected selection of analytical categories or in the planning of teaching units. History didactician Bernd-Stefan Grewe comments:

> We have to think fundamentally about whether a concept coined in and for Europe implicitly contains normative ideas and whether it can be applied universally at all, i.e. also to non-European contexts. (Grewe 2016, 310)

How to avoid falling into the trap of *methodological nationalism* when planning teaching units and reflect the spatial dimension in the structuring of history education instead, is shown by Vadim Oswalt in his handbook 'Planung von Unterrichtseinheiten. Wie man Geschichte (an)ordnen kann' ('Planning Teaching Units. How to Arrange History') (Oswalt 2016).

However, turning away from *methodological nationalism* does not mean that the nation or the nation-state should no longer be given attention. This criticism at the methodological level should not be understood as a plea that the nation state has become obsolete. In the past as well as in the present, nation states form a powerful unit that centrally influences the political organization of many societies, knowledge systems and much more. Current political developments such as Brexit or the increasing influence of right-wing parties indicate that we are not approaching a decline of the nation-state model, as many voices predicted in the context of the globalization debate. María do Mar Castro Varela and Alisha Heinemann rather see a "neo-patriotic age" imminent (Castro Varela and Heinemann 2017, 41-42). For this reason, the national framework certainly remains a relevant reference for a large number of questions. Whereby the development of the global horizon of national historical events should not be forgotten.

To deal with a *methodological nationalism* in history didactics means to question the subject fundamentally, and also to deal with the possible unwanted side effects of the classical national chronology in history education (Völkel 2013). The consideration of *de-centering* history education is a contribution to this outstanding debate. It is not a question of an all-encompassing turnaround, but rather an integrative approach that aims to promote entangled historical thinking and is related to the existing framework conditions of schools. Certainly, a perspective of historical entanglements should not be overused in school education. After all, global context is not always and everywhere fundamental and not everything is interwoven and entangled. Rather, there are questions that require a turn in global history more than others (Conrad 2013, 27). If we only try to think about historical change globally, there is also the danger of losing sight of local or national dynamics (Grewe 2016, 314). Instead, it is a matter of promoting an entangled spatial-historical way of thinking which can be integrated into conventional history education by starting from the classical, national-historical oriented topics of the curriculum. This proposition ties in with Susanne Popp's approach of a world and global historical perspective. Popp notes:

> If one places 'world history' unconnectedly next to a national history that trades as 'our own' history, that history inevitably represents a history of the 'non-us', instead of the national 'own history' being classified into comprehensive 'world-historical' developments. Therefore, this arrangement misses the decisive factor: It does not promote the change of perspective which perceives the 'own history' once in the familiar inner perspective, but then also in a world-historical macro-perspective. (Popp 2005, 493)

This approach can be connected to a spatial reference level of *Entangled History*, which does not understand the global level as separate from the national or local ones, but looks at global entanglements, interactions and exchange processes that manifest themselves locally. Instead of replacing a national narrative with a global one, an approach of global entanglements is intended to promote interconnected historical thinking and thereby consciously reflect the spatial level of reference. In order to learn to think global entanglements historically, the step proposed by Popp to contrast a national inner perspective with a global macro-perspective seems essential. This approach can be further developed and expanded through impulses from Entangled History. Popp chooses the double term "*world- and global-historical perspectivation.*" With G*lobal History* Popp refers to the history of globalization. In order to not restrict the desired "transregional and transcultural broadening of horizons" to globalization, which could be limited in time, she adds the concept of *"world-historical perspectivation."* This refers to a spatial broadening of the horizon encompassing the globe. The aim is "to familiarize students with a macro-perspective on a global scale" (Popp 2005, 494). I, on the other hand, want to plead for a wider definition of the concept of *Global History* and not to limit it to the history of globalization. Rather, I understand the history of globalization as a branch of *Global History*, which shows a special focus and its own questions (see also Conrad 2013, 19). In the debate about Global Education in schools, to me the strong focus on globalization seems problematic. Because if the efforts to bring global perspectives into the classroom move only between a teleological narrative of progressive interconnection (Conrad 2013, 13) on the one hand and global crises on the other, then the global perspective imparted by this is quite one-sided. It is also important to me to show that a global historical perspectivation is not necessarily the same as a macro-perspective. At this point, the historiographical examination of the debates on S*patial Turn* and the central quotation of Karl Schlögel can be referred to. "There is no story in nowhere. Everything has a beginning and an end. All history has a place." (Schlögel 2016 [2003], 71)

And in this sense, global connections can be found specifically in the local. In the same way at one's own doorstep, in one's everyday life; as well as in distant places of the world, in other people's everyday lives, in the present and also in the past. The sociologist Roland Robertson already coined the term *Glocalization* in the 1990s in order to draw attention to a mutual interpenetration of global and local contexts (Beck 1989, 88-94). Castro Varela and Heinemann conclude subsequent to Robertson:

> The global can always be identified in the local, just as the local is no longer readable without the global. Translated into educational policy, this would mean that any education is necessarily also global. (Castro Varela and Heinemann 2017, 41-42)

Based on local manifestations of the global, recent global historical approaches make global perspectives not only empirical, but also tangible for school education. Classically, Global Education also draws on this idea, which is often expressed in the slogan "think global, act local." Teaching materials on Global Education often start with everyday commodities and trace their global production chain. Here, for example, one can refer to the teaching materials of Welthaus (World house) Bielefeld e.V., which make the production process of cocoa tangible with all senses (BildungsBag SchokoExpedition) or trace the global economy on the production chain and the long journey of a pair of jeans (Welthaus Bielefeld 2013).

- In his essay 'Unbounded Spaces and the Localization of the Global'[22] (2016), Bernd-Stefan Grewe demonstrates this procedure for history education through the example of a cocoa pot from the Couven Museum in Aachen and uses it to point out the close connection between European consumption history, colonialism and the slave trade.

- The historical didactician Lars Deile proceeds in a similar way and traces – starting from an everyday object, a comb of the traditional Hamburg company Hercules Sägemann – conflicts over rubber cultivation in the Amazon region in the 19th and 20th centuries (Barricelli et al. 2018).

---

22 'Entgrenzte Räume und die Verortung des Globalen'.

- The publication 'Colonialism and Decolonization in National Historical Cultures and Remembrance Policies in Europe'[23] contains modules for history education on European colonialism in the late 18th century. These started with potatoes, coffee and sugar and show how these non-European imports have changed the continent. Or use the example of a Swiss emigrant family to point out the European involvement with the slave economy in Brazil (Fenske et al. 2015).

- This ambivalent European modernity, whose dark sides – colonial rule and slavery – are far too often not addressed, is also the subject of the teaching folder 'Respect, Honor, Merit? The Upmanns. The Story of a Global Family Business'[24]. The unit is based on individual stages in the corporate history of the Bielefeld merchant family, which achieved great wealth and prestige through a tobacco manufactory, and calls on the students themselves to make a historical-political judgment (Frey 2019).

5.2. Overcoming Eurocentrism

In the debate about *Global History*, one-sided, Eurocentric perspectives are questioned and approaches to understand global events as a kind of diffusion of European achievements into the world – as older world-historical approaches have often done – are criticized. Sebastian Conrad notes in this regard that global historical works today clearly distance themselves from this understanding of "world history as a one-way street" and instead emphasize the "relational dimension of historical processes", pointing out the significance of interactions and exchange (Conrad 2013, 22-23).

---

23 'Kolonialismus und Dekolonisation in nationalen Geschichtskulturen und Erinnerungspolitiken in Europa'.

24 'Respekt, Ehre, Verdienst? Die Upmanns. Geschichte eines globalen Familienunternehmens'.

Last but not least, European development cannot be explained autonomously; it was also integrated into different contexts of interaction. (Conrad 2013, 22-23)

The first edition of the anthology 'Beyond Eurocentrism'[25], published in 2002 by Sebastian Conrad, Shalini Randeria and from the second edition also by Regina Römhild, formulates a clear criticism of the idea that European modernity is an independent development detached from the rest of the world (Conrad and Randeria 2013, 33). Thus a progress history of the West is questioned, which interprets the history of Europe as a separate and self-created development (Conrad and Randeria 2013, 35). To illustrate these thoughts, Regina Römhild and Shalini Randeria quote the cultural theorist Stuart Hall, born in Kingston – Jamaica, in the introduction to the anthology. He is one of Britain's leading cultural theorists and his work is regarded as a central point of reference for anti-colonial and anti-imperialist movements.

> People like me who came to England in the 1950s have been there for centuries. I was coming home. I am the sugar on the bottom of the English cup of tea. (…) This is the symbolization of English identity. (…) Where does it come from? Ceylon – Sri Lanka, India. That is the outside history that is inside the history of the English. There's no English story without that other history. (Hall 2017, 74)

Through such a relational perspective, the discussion about modernity is critically repositioned. In recent years, global historical works such as Sven Beckert's 'King Cotton' (Beckert 2015) have picked up such theoretical premises empirically and made them tangible. In his work, Beckert analyzes the capitalist world economy using the example of cotton as the central resource and empirically investigates the connections between imperialism and industrialization. In this way, global historical works show completely new approaches to well-known topics central to history education, such as the industrial revolution.

---

25   'Jenseits des Eurozentrismus'.

- In the source book 'Global Perspectives in History Education'[26] (2010) published by Klett-Verlag, Wolfgang Geiger makes the examination of the commodity cotton, global division of labor and industrialization tangible for history education.

- How a non-Eurocentric approach to history teaching can look like, is also demonstrated in the teaching folder 'Cold War in Latin America'[27]. The materials focus on protagonists who do not find attention in a Eurocentric view of the Cold War (Petersen 2018).

Following on from these thoughts, *Eurocentrism* is described as a perspective that comprehends the historical development of Western Europe and North America as a universal model that provides a benchmark for all other societies and their historical and contemporary processes. For such a comparison goes hand in hand with a deficient perspective. Differences inevitably become deficits (Conrad and Randeria 2013, 35). Shalini Randeria juxtaposes one-sided, Eurocentric narratives with the concept of a *Shared History*. It is about the development of a transnational approach to the analysis of a modernity understood as entangled. An approach that looks at commonalities, entanglement and togetherness as well as differences, breaches and demarcations (Conrad and Randeria 2013, 62).

> The term 'Shared Histories' goes (...) conceptually beyond the emphasis on historical commonalities. The manifold interactions produced not only a divided/common history, but at the same time demarcations and breaches. On the one hand, this concerns numerous differences and inequalities within societies, but also differentiations between the nation states. (Conrad and Randeria 2013, 41)

In German, the term "geteilt" (divided) is an ambiguity that could be expressed in the English translation by the terms *shared* and *di-*

---

26 'Globale Perspektiven im Geschichtsunterricht'.
27 'Kalter Krieg in Lateinamerika'.

vided. The term consequently captures the ambivalences of a history of interaction and exchange. A history which is at the same time a shared one in the sense of a common, as well as a divided one in the sense of a separate, different or separating experience.

> On the one hand, one can read the emergence and development of the modern world as a 'common history' in which different cultures and societies shared a number of central experiences and through their interactions and interdependencies constituted the modern world together. On the other hand, the increasing circulation of goods, people and ideas produced not only similarities, but at the same time demarcations [...]. (Conrad and Randeria 2013, 39-40)

The purpose is not a mere reversal of the Eurocentric perspective, but a *de-centering* of the "West" as an unquestioned benchmark, moreover a critique of a teleological, self-referential history of modernism (Conrad and Randeria 2013, 36). Instead, it is proposed to think of modern history as "an ensemble of entanglements" and to overcome a tunnel vision that derives the history of Europe or a nation from itself (Conrad and Randeria 2013, 40). Randeria advocates a relational approach and the focusing on interactions between the non-European world and Europe (Conrad and Randeria 2013, 37). Such an understanding of European modernism and the history of colonialism as two sides of the same coin, represents the core of postcolonial and decolonial theories (Mignolo 2000). A *de-centering* of the West also means a detachment from binary category systems and last but not least, a departure from a closed understanding of culture. In this sense, Homi Bhabha advocates for an open and dynamic understanding of culture. Instead of conceiving cultures in the past or present as static and naturally given categories, he emphasizes processes of negotiation and construction of culture and identity. Against this background, the tendency of many multi- and intercultural approaches that attempt to homogenize disparate cultures can be criticized (Castro Varela and Dhawan 2015, 247).

- The authors of the volume 'Transcultural History Didactics'[28] (Wagner-Kyora, Wilczek, and Huneke 2008) show how an open and hybrid understanding of culture can find its place in history education instead.

Perspectives from Global and Entangled History change the direction of the questions and shift the view to the past. However, the degree of abstraction of these theoretical considerations does not always make it easy to translate them directly into history education. Roland Wenzlhuemer accuses *Global History* of having dealt insufficiently with the character of entanglements and connections "and of having done so without enough precision, without enough analytical differentiation" (Wenzlhuemer 2017, 21). The openness and range of perspectives from *Global* and *Entangled History* is interesting for the orientation of our own research. For the establishment of global historical perspectives in history education, still, this poses a difficulty. It is necessary to specify how global entanglements can be comprehended, how global relations differ from regional or local ones, for example. The transfer of these discussions into teaching practice is therefore a challenge which should not be underestimated and that a didactic of history cannot master alone.

5.3. De-Centering the Curriculum

The entry of global historical approaches into the curriculum discussion quickly leads to the general problem of selection that history has to deal with. Every historiographical research is shaped by its specific point of view; an objective overall picture is nearly impossible. If one follows the avoidance of global historical approaches from a nation-state tunnel vision, the question arises as to which selection criteria can be applied in view of the wealth of content resulting from global historical expansion. The critique of a traditional chronological history education, which reduces "the" history to a

---

28   'Transkulturelle Geschichtsdidaktik'.

Western-European tradition context from Greek antiquity via the Romans to the "modern world" and thus marginalizes other stories, raises the question of alternatives to such a chronology.

Do we follow the poststructuralist postulate of the "end of the great narratives" or do we need a new master narrative in the age of globalization? In his much-quoted work 'Local Histories/Global Designs', the decolonial theorist Walter Mignolo pleads for a *different way of thinking* beyond linear Western concepts of time. A way of thinking that results from the spatial confrontation of different local historical narratives and reflects on power structures (Mignolo 2000). In formulating alternatives to hegemonic, colonial discourses, he advocates changing the structures of knowledge production.

> Macronarratives from the perspective of coloniality are precisely the places in which 'an other thinking' could be implemented, not in order to tell the truth over lies, but to think otherwise, to move towards 'an other logic' – in sum, to change the terms, not just the content of the conversation. Such narratives make it possible to think coloniality, and not only modernity, at large. The epistemological implementations are enormous. (Mignolo 2000, 69-70)

In this sense, the following practical approaches should not only be understood as a shift in content, but rather as a fundamental shift in perspective. The approaches presented are intended to illustrate in an exemplary way, how such a shift can look like. At best, they can stimulate a discussion and give an impulse to rethink beyond the specific proposals. Mignolo also raises the idea of creating alternative macronarratives that enable a different logic of knowledge production. In the following, this idea of the alternative macronarrative for history teaching, which Mignolo did not concretize, will be discussed. In this context, Susanne Popp's reflections on a world and global historical perspective, within the framework of the current history curricula in the Federal Republic of Germany, will be continued. The approach presented above is based on well-known, mandatory topics in history education and aims to step out of a *nation-centered* inner perspective. In this sense, the examination of non-

European history is not added additively, but leads to a different approach to topics that were previously only viewed from the local or national inner perspective (Popp 2005, 502). The advantage of this approach lies in the fact that the students are repeatedly made aware of the location dependent nature of a historical narrative in order to counteract an idea of history as a linear development. For this to succeed, an attempt should be made to actively involve the students in the reflection of the spatial references shown. A central didactic function of this approach is a "metacognitive modelling of historical learning processes." Popp explains:

> The historical cosmos that the school subject history (and even more the 'field' history in subject groups) presents to the students, resembles, to use a picture of Lyotard, a world of islands where a ferry travels only very rarely between them. The metacognitive function of world and global historical perspectives now consists, on the one hand, in integrating individual topics into a certain overarching context, and, on the other hand, in sounding out the limits of the knowledge presented in the classroom to a greater extent than before. (Popp 2005, 506)

According to Popp, a first step towards the systematic establishment of a global historical perspective in history education consists in

> identifying certain historical phases of historical developments at the macro level and examining whether and to what extent, they are at all connectable and suitable for the construction of world and global historical perspectives on 'local' topics. (Popp 2005, 503)

In order to locate the relevant historical phases at the macro level and not to get stuck in a Eurocentric perspective, reference is made below to the discussions on the Routledge Handbook 'History and Society of the Americas' (2019). The handbook presents key issues related to social and historical developments in the Americas from an inter-American perspective. In the introduction, the editors address the conceptual debates about the structure of the volume and attempt to create a historical contextualization that links the individual contributions. To this end, they evaluate different approaches to an entanglement historical inter-American contextualization. In order to set themselves apart from traditional event-historical approaches – and because they particularly want to emphasize processual and often opposing dynamics, continuities and breaches – a timeline with chronologically arranged events does not seem suitable for contextualization to the authors. In contrast, contextualization through historical conjunctures from a global historical perspective is more appropriate to include different developments. On the other hand, there is the trap of suggesting a comprehensive and coherent dynamic of these conjunctures. Thus, the problem of a homogenization of quite diverse tendencies by the overemphasis of the common (Kaltmeier 2019, 6). They are therefore taking a third approach, which emphasizes historical changes and breaches in history.

These conceptual considerations follow on from the German historian Reinhart Koselleck. He coined the term *Sattelzeit* (according to the image of a mountain saddle) to describe an epoch threshold or transitional period between early modern times and modernism. According to Koselleck, the period from about 1750 to 1850 was marked by such profound political, social and cultural changes that concepts with a long semantic tradition dating back to antiquity changed their significance dramatically. Therefore, after the French Revolution, a fundamental change of importance took place. The authors take up this idea of *Sattelzeit*, which marks a social upheaval or a turning point, and from there develop a conceptual approach to their own historical contextualization, which they think starting from the Americas. They take this idea of Koselleck's upheaval conceptually, but do not transfer Koselleck's division into epochs to the Americas but discuss the turning points from an interAmerican perspective. For the Americas, the year 1492 represents a fundamental turning point on a macro level. This moment marks a cultural meeting of Europe, Asia and Africa in the western hemisphere and represents the starting point for the emergence of a capitalist world system. As a result, different indigenous worldviews are destroyed or fundamentally changed (Kaltmeier 2019, 6).

After this profound caesura, however, the authors shift their *Turning Points* to a meso-level of historical conjunctures that follow one another more closely. The density of these turning points seems to have a potential to sharpen a sense of change and temporality in history education. If we look at the *Turning Points* that the authors define, it is noticeable that they overlap in many places with turning points that can be defined from Europe. Hence, the entangled and re-lational character of different local historical developments becomes clear. Furthermore, it can be emphasized that the *Turning Points* are often not characterized by a specific global event, but that at these turning points very different dynamics solidify. In the following table these interAmerican turning points are listed, as well as a keyword-like outlook on different developments, which solidify on these.[29]

InterAmerican Turning Points	
1492	• Meeting of Europe, Asia and Africa in the Western Hemi-sphere
1898	• End of the Spanish-American War
1917	• Mexican Revolution • Entry of the USA into the First World War (Zimmermann-Depesche) • Russian Revolution • Social-revolutionary movements (e.g. first women's move-ments)
1948	• Establishment of a bipolar world order after the Second World War • End of the Good Neighbor Policy and interventionist US for-eign policy in Latin America • National liberation movements (social revolutions in Bolivia 1952 & Cuba 1959)

---

29 This exemplary list refers to the introductions and historical contex-tualization of the Routledge Handbook 'History and Society of the Americas' (2019).

1968-73	• Increasing confrontation of social-revolutionary and reactionary-capitalist political forces • Worldwide social movement (e.g. against US intervention in Vietnam) • Social movements in Latin America are stopped by violence (e.g.the movement of 1968 in Mexico/Massacre of Tlatelolco & military coup in Chile 1973) • Neoconservative backlash
1989/90	• Invention of the Internet • "Democratization wave" in Latin America • End of the Cold War

If we follow Susanne Popp's approach of global historical perspectivation, we have to – besides just identifying historical phases on the macro level (where historical turning points were identified) – distinguish keywords to link local perspectives with the macro level, (Popp 2005, 503). When identifying such topics, a certain openness should be taken into account in order to leave the necessary space for other perspectives and approaches. The list above could contribute to such a discussion. However, there is a need both for different regional scientific perspectives and for a fundamental discussion about the character of the keywords of history education oriented towards global history. How can a *nation-centric* and *euro-centric* perspective be overcome? Which categories and concepts are beneficial to a global perspective? In addition, this discussion should be linked back to the existing curriculum topics and the question should be asked, how these classical subject areas can be viewed from a global history perspective.

5.4. A View from Latin America

Finally, the example of the upheavals around 1989/90 will be used to show how a global historical turning point of a well-known field of history education can look in specific terms. The epoch year will be viewed from Latin America, with a focus on political developments in Chile. 1989 is a classic topic in school education. A global dynamic is inherent in the 1989 nodal point. However, the field of content in school education is mostly viewed from a *nation-centered* inner perspective, as can be very clearly seen from the example of the curriculum for history of the state of North Rhine Westphalia (secondary education II grammar school & comprehensive school). The topic can be found in this curriculum in the field of "Nationalism, nation-state and German identity in the 19th and 20th centuries." The curriculum focuses on "overcoming the German division in the peaceful revolution of 1989." The classification of the global epoch year 1989 under the topic of the nation-state and German identity seems to be a prime example of a national tunnel vision. This classification cuts out the global dimension of the upheavals around 1989/90. After all, in reference to the competences to be acquired there is an indication that leads to a global historical classification. It points to an explanation of the peaceful revolution of 1989 and the development from the fall of the Berlin Wall to German Unity in the context of national and international conditional factors.

Below, the example of the upheavals around 1989/90 will show how a global historical turnaround of a curriculum topic could look like. This contribution was developed in the course of the conference (2019) of the working group 'World and Global Historical Perspectives'[30] of the Conference for History Didactics (KGD) about the upheavals of 1989 viewed from a Global Historical Perspective. The aim of the working group is to anchor more global perspectives in history education (Weber 2019).

The call for papers to the conference made me think, and in particular I asked myself some questions: What does epoch year actually mean? What makes such a turning point year? How does an upheaval become a global turnaround? What makes such a caesura in "the" history? What history are we talking about here? And what breach does 1989 actually represent? Not only people in Germany

---

30 'Welt und globalgeschichtliche Perspektiven'.

have the image of celebrating people on the Berlin Wall in their minds.

The end of the East-West conflict represents a turning point for global power relations, for some it is a symbol of freedom and democracy. What does it mean if we talk about globalizing such an epoch year? Then, what is it about? It would be possible to begin to trace the effects of this drastic event in other parts of the world and to uncover interactions with other events. One will inevitably encounter other perceptions of the end of the confrontation of the Blocs, other interpretations of history. But until where do we go when it comes to placing the epoch year 1989 in a global context? And what happens if we come across things that do not fit into our search grid. How "different" may the other perspective be, so that it still fits to our ambition? And does the selected nodal point even have the potential to enable a horizontal dialogue at all? Or is this too narrowly defined or too strongly connected to the end of the Cold War and does not even allow other dynamics to be taken into consideration? And is 1989 seen from Latin America a turning point at all?

To understand 1989 as a nodal point of a global oriented history education, which allows an extension of the view and a way out of the national tunnel vision, seems to be a promising starting point to me. Learning to think about historical entanglements is still an unfulfilled but fundamental task of history education. This goes hand in hand with an examination of multi-perspectivity in an intertwined world marked by global asymmetries. 'A View from Latin America' is the title of my lecture, this refers to a relocation or a de-centralization. In my contribution, I want to concentrate on reviewing the upheavals around the year 1989 from another location, and on developing a certain openness that also allows considering other dynamics and upheavals of the threshold between 1989 and 1990. What happens if we try to look at 1989 from the Latin American perspective?

Historian David Campbell once wrote that the Cold War "needs to be understood as a disciplinary strategy that was global in scope but national in design" (Campbell 1998, 153). This statement can be extended to the end of the Cold War. The global dimension of this geopolitical upheaval mixes with certain local conflicts. The following draft will attempt to understand this spatial entanglement and not to subordinate the local perspectives, but to see them as constitutive for the global dimension. I would like to concretize my theoretical considerations in the conceptual planning of a teaching unit for history education.

For this purpose, reference is made to the contextualization of the Routledge Handbook 'History and Society of the Americas' (2019), presented above. In view of the interAmerican orientation of this essay, this seems to be a useful orientation. The aim here is not so much to create an all-encompassing contribution, but rather to bring the own expertise from the regional studies on Latin America into the discussion. The convention of the working group of the Conference for History Didactics made clear how diverse and versatile approaches to the main topic of 1989 can be. The upheavals around 1989/90, seen from the Americas, can be defined as a global turning point by different developments. A profound impact was caused by developments in the field of information technology, mainly the invention of the World Wide Web in 1989. Also the developments in the field of biotechnology (in particular the field of genetic engineering) provoked immense changes and conflicts in agriculture. These technological innovations coincide with the end of the socialist Bloc as an alternative to the capitalist system, leading to a shift in global power relations (Kaltmeier, Stewart Foley, and Rufer 2019, 216-17).

In the context of this global crisis of socialism, socialist governments in Latin America had to struggle with their own problems: The Sandinistas in Nicaragua, a model country for socialist (or left-wing) politics beyond the Soviet way, lost the 1990 elections to the conservative Violeta Chamorro, who represented an anti-Sandinist party alliance backed by the USA. Cuba, the country with the closest ties to the Soviet Union, was on the verge of economic collapse. It certainly makes sense to place these developments in a larger context and, of course, interactions and interdependencies can also be observed here. Let's take the example of Cuba. In 1989, Cuba still handled 85% of its foreign trade via the socialist Eastern Bloc states. It is obvious that the upheavals in Eastern Europe had an effect on the country's economic development. In addition to such hard facts, the upheavals in Eastern Europe also had a big impact on a discursive level. Thus the end of the Soviet system raised the question of an end of socialism as utopia and caused many Latin American intellectuals to think about it. Further, a third development is to be focused on, which represents a regional proprietary development. With regards to Latin America, 1989/90 also represents a turning point towards a new wave of democratization (Kaltmeier, Stewart Foley, and Rufer 2019, 217). This usually means a transition from autocratic regimes to democracies with free elections. The end of the Pinochet dictatorship in Chile is a prime example of this democratization. I will go into this case study in more detail below. After a referendum on the continuation of the dictatorship and subsequent free elections, the Christian democrat Patricio Aylwin took office as President in 1990. The dictatorships in Argentina (1983) and Uruguay (1985) had already come to an end. In Brazil, a military dictatorship that lasted almost twenty-nine years ended in 1985. The dictatorship of Alfredo Stroessner in Paraguay ended in 1993. In Central America, free elections have been held successively since the mid-1980s. In the context of the Cold War and through the intervention of the USA, which had supported oligarchic regimes in the region, there had been violent clashes and civil wars in El Salvador, Honduras, Guatemala and Nicaragua in the sixties (Thiery 2007).

To describe this wave of democratization in Latin America, one also speaks of a domino effect. The framework of this regional economy is a turnaround of the USA, which supported the military dictatorships in the region during the height of the Cold War. Nevertheless, the own dynamics of the respective societies are particularly decisive for these processes (Thiery 2007). In order to be able to capture them, however, we have to leave the macro level in which I have argued so far. Exemplarily, I would like to develop in further detail the case of Chile. This elaboration on the upheavals in Chile around 1989/90 is accompanied by source material which I deem interesting for a teaching unit.

In 1973, the military organized a coup against the socialist government of Salvador Allende. The bombing of the presidential palace represents a radical breach in the history of the country. The last radio address by Salvador Allende shortly before the bombing represents a snapshot of this historic rupture (Allende 1973). In the historical and cultural processing of this past and the memory of the terror of the military dictatorship, this source represents a central document. Thousands of socialists, communists or political dissenters of any kind are subsequently murdered, "disappeared"[31] or have to flee into exile. Many of them lived or still live in Germany today. The terror during the early years was subsequently replaced by the institutionalization of military rule. In the junta, the protagonists who demanded a radical liberalization of the economy had prevailed. The American economist Milton Friedman and the so-called Chicago Boys (Chilean economists trained in the USA) advised the military during this period. The constitution of 1980, which is still mostly enforced today, seals the political and economic path of the military junta. Today's conflicts over the privatization of education, pension and health insurance or environmental conflicts over the right to water, result from this recent past and constitutional principles that still stem from the military dictatorship. Compared to other dictatorships in Latin America, the Pinochet dictatorship achieved a remarkable institutionalization and was supported by about one third of the population. These circumstances led to the fact that the regime could steer the transition to democracy and determine the conditions (Thiery 2007). Therefore, the end of the dictatorship in

---

31   The term "disappeared" refers here to the term *Detenidos Desaparecidos* (Spanish). This is a practice of state repression against opposition members who are secretly kidnapped or arrested, tortured and murdered.

Chile was characterized in particular by the voluntary transfer of power from the authoritarian elites. Under international pressure, the military rule became increasingly difficult to legitimize, and since the beginning of the 1980s, there had been massive protests by the opposition. So, the regime chose the option of a referendum to confirm its own rulership. In 1988, the population was given a referendum to decide whether or not to vote out the military government. The opposition alliance, which launched a major campaign with the slogan "NO!" against the military government, won the referendum narrowly (Junge 2014, 130).[32] Subsequently, elections were permitted with the participation of the opposition alliance of center-left parties (*Concertación por la Democracia*) which managed to obtain the majority of votes (Moulian 1997, 216-18). The Christian democrat Patricio Aylwin took office as President in 1990. Although Plan A would have certainly been to win this referendum themselves, defeat did not mean that the conservative elites, who led the military dictatorship, lost their areas of power. Through legal requirements or constitutional mechanisms (also referred to as *Authoritarian Enclaves*), they had secured their power by thinking ahead (Junge 2014, 130).

The Chilean sociologist Thomas Moulian calls this a strategy of *transformismo* in his work 'Chile actual. Anatomía de un mito'. In it, he describes regime change as a process that was already initiated during the military dictatorship and was also intended to guarantee the continued power of the authoritarian and right-wing conservative elites in the post-dictatorial order (Moulian 1997, 145). By forcing the opposition to recognize the 1980 constitution, the military government paved the way for the post-dictatorship and established a political system that ensured the continuity of the neoliberal socio-

---

32   The feature film "NO!" by director Pablo Larraín, released in 2012, gives a good overview of this first phase of transition. The film is based on a play by the Chilean writer Antonio Skármeta and incorporates commercials from the plebiscite campaigns and archive footage.

economic model (Moulian 1997, 147). The *Concertación*, which provided the government for twenty years, succeeded in abolishing individual authoritarian enclaves. However, this did not alter the continuity of the neoliberal model, especially through the influence of protagonists from the private sector and political spectrum who propagated the irreversibility of this economic policy path (Junge 2014, 132-33).

Due to these structural continuities, many people do not even perceive the transition as a democratization process. Moreover, the general feeling is that basic social rights have still been deprived. In addition, the revision of the dictatorship's human rights crimes, has been slow and in some cases not been completed to date. The recent social movements in Chile, the massive protests of students and an enormous social movement for a reform of the pension system are representative of this unease. One source that shows this mood quite well is an interview with Valentina Saavedra. In 2015, she was the spokesperson for the National Confederation of Chilean Students. In the interview she explains how the massive student protests of 2011 came about, the biggest protests since the end of the dictatorship. Here's an excerpt:

> [...] for twenty years one could govern this country with the promise of social mobility, joy, democracy and since the 2010s one begins to understand that these promises have not been fulfilled, that there is no democracy, no right, and certainly no joy in society. (Valentina Saavedra, here quoted after Schwabe 2017, 45)

While Valentina and many other young people in Chile draw attention to the consequences of the radical and far-reaching liberalization of the economy made possible by the dictatorship, for others this economic restructuring is an example. Due to the new geopolitical situation after the end of the Cold War, with the USA as the leading world power, other countries are following this economic path. The liberalization of the economy and free trade agreements mark the period after 1989. It seems interesting to emphasize that Chile was also a point of orientation for liberal economists in the former socialist countries. In their eyes, Chile was an example of how an economically and politically catastrophically positioned country can achieve economic recovery and an excellent macroeconomic balance sheet. Yet, authoritarian rule as the basis of a successful economy does not seem to have been perceived as a contradiction at all, as shown by the short report entitled 'Pinochet as a Role Model'[33] in the newspaper *Neues Deutschland*. It quotes Vladimir Putin, the second mayor of Saint Petersburg at the time and current president of Russia. The author of the article is outraged by its attitude:

> Putin distinguished between 'necessary' and 'criminal' violence. Political violence is 'criminal' if it is aimed at eliminating market-economy conditions, 'necessary' if it promotes or protects private capital investments. He, Putin, expressly approved Yeltsin's and the military's preparations for the establishment of a dictatorship modeled on Pinochet in view of the difficult private sector path. Putin's remarks were warmly applauded both by the German company representatives and by the Deputy German Consul General present. (Neues Deutschand 1993)

A source that makes global entanglements tangible, like few other sources. Not only in Chile, but also in many other Latin American countries, the formal transition to democracy is not satisfactory for many social protagonists. In the early 1990s this was clearly demonstrated by the emergence of new social protests. These responded to the consolidation of global neoliberal free trade regimes. In addition to the strengthening of an anti-globalization movement and increased awareness of environmental issues, Latin America saw a new wave of indigenous protests on the occasion of the 500th anniversary of 1492, which led to constitutional changes in numerous countries (such as Colombia, Peru, Bolivia and Ecuador). New protagonists entered the political arena and challenged the existing political systems. The protests not only drew attention to the fact that

---

33   'Pinochet als Vorbild'.

democratic participation does not exist for all population groups, but also questioned the foundations of the existing democratic systems and put them to the test.

Those protests should be considered when we think about the wave of democratization in Latin America around 1989. Consideration within an open approach that also allows us to look at other dynamics, dynamics that we may have not looked for at all, the existence of which we may not even have been aware of. This is what horizontal dialogue and reciprocity mean. The prerequisite is the willingness to change one's own limited perspective or one's *own*.

Against this background, I would therefore like to emphasize, once again, the question raised at the beginning: What do we actually mean when we speak of 1989 as a global nodal point? It is always important to reflect whether such a nodal point has the unifying function of representing a point of dialogue at all.

6. Concluding Remarks

The present text has shown how the demand for a *de-centering* of historical learning is theoretically justified. At the same time, practical starting points for history education were presented. However, the project of *de-centering* is far from being implemented and the idea is far from being finished. Rather, it requires the continuation of a dialogue on the possibilities of a global historical perspectivation of historical learning. Expertise from the regional sciences is an important part of this. But there is also a need, on the part of historical didactics, for further self-reflection of one's own discipline. So far, too little has been thought about spatial references or world designs of historical didactics. Even though there have been moments in the historical didactic discourse in the past, when the national identity was questioned.

Additionally, there were repeatedly discussions in history didactics about European and non-European spaces and societies. These perspectives on the world, as well as the world designs of historical didactics, change in the course of time and are in a reciprocal relationship to geo-political and socio-political discourses. A confrontation with world designs of the past could form an orientation for action in the present, also because the confrontation with these historical perspectives, which are mostly foreign today, permits a deeper consideration of the object. At the same time, the question of the creation of the present offers a possibility of social self-reflection. Because the fact that something has been forgotten does not mean that it no longer exists. Instead, the production of knowledge is based on an (often only implicitly visible and mostly unconscious) understanding of the world. Corresponding assumptions shape our perception of the past and what we tell about it. Pierre Bourdieu notes in his reflections on sociology of sociologists in his work 'Esquisses algériennes'[34]:

---

34 'Algerische Skizzen'.

The unconscious, this is forgetting history. The unconscious of a discipline is, I think, its history; the unconscious are the hidden, forgotten social conditions of production: the product separated from its social conditions of production undergoes a change of meaning and has an ideological effect. (Bourdieu 2010, 445)

In this sense and in the context of rising right-wing ideologies, sociology of ourselves as history didactics, as well as a discussion of worldviews and identity references in history education is more than overdue. This could be a foundation for a deeper *de-centering* of history education.

Works Cited

Abelein, Werner, ed. 2010. *Globale Perspektiven im Geschichtsunterricht: Texte und Quellen in Auswahl.* Tempora – Quellen zur Geschichte und Politik. Stuttgart: Klett.

Allende, Salvador. 1973. "Último discurso de Salvador Allende Gossens, transmitido por Radio Magallanes desde el Palacio de La Moneda durante el golpe de Estado del 11 de septiembre de 1973." In *Wikisource.* https://es.wikisource.org/wiki/%C3%9 Altima_alocuci%C3%B3n_de_Salvador_Allende.

Asbrand, Barbara and Anette Scheunpflug. 2014. "Globales Lernen." In *Handbuch politische Bildung*, ed. Wolfgang Sander, 4th ed., 401-414. Schwalbach/Ts: Wochenschau Verlag.

Barricelli, Michele, Lars Deile, Olaf Kaltmeier, Jochen Kemner, Susanne Popp and Jörg van Norden. 2018. *Globalgeschichtliche Perspektiven und Globales Lernen im Geschichtsunterricht. Konzeptionelle Überlegungen.* Bielefeld: Kipu.

Bauck, Sönke and Thomas Maier. 2015. "Entangled History." In *InterAmerican Wiki: Terms – Concepts – Critical Perspectives.* www.uni-bielefeld.de/cias/wiki/e_Entangled_History.html.

Bauman, Zygmunt. 2016. *Die Angst vor den anderen: Ein Essay über Migration und Panikmache.* Berlin: Suhrkamp.

Beck, Ulrich. 1998. *Was ist Globalisierung? Irrtümer des Globalismus – Antworten auf Globalisierung.* 5th ed. Frankfurt am Main: Suhrkamp.

Beckert, Sven. 2015. *King Cotton: Eine Geschichte des globalen Kapitalismus.* 2nd ed. München: C.H. Beck.

Belina, Bernd and Boris Michel, eds. 2007. "Raumproduktionen. Zu diesem Band." In *Raumproduktionen: Beiträge der Radical Geography. Eine Zwischenbilanz*, 7-35. Münster: Westfälisches Dampfboot.

Benke, Karlheinz. 2005. *Geographie(n) der Kinder: von Räumen und Grenzen (in) der Postmoderne.* Forum Sozialwissenschaften 2. München: m press.

BMU, ed. 2018. *Zukunft? Jugend Fragen! Nachhaltigkeit, Politik, Engagement – Eine Studie zu Einstellungen und Alltag junger Menschen.* https://www.bmu.de/fileadmin/Daten_BMU/Pools/ Broschueren/jugendstudie_bf.pdf.

Borries, Bodo von. 2008. *Historisch denken lernen – Welterschließung statt Epochenüberblick: Geschichte als Unterrichtsfach und Bildungsaufgabe.* Studien zur Bildungsgangforschung 21. Opladen: Budrich.

Bourdieu, Pierre. 2010. *Algerische Skizzen.* Translated by Tassadit Yacine-Titouh, Andreas Pfeuffer, Achim Russer, and Bernd Schwibs. Berlin: Suhrkamp.

Calmbach, Marc, Silke Borgstedt, Inga Borchard, Peter Martin Thomas, and Berthold Bodo Flaig. 2016. *Wie ticken Jugendliche 2016? Lebenswelten von Jugendlichen im Alter von 14 bis 17 Jahren in Deutschland.* Ed. SINUS Markt- und Sozialforschung GmbH. Wiesbaden: Springer.

Campbell, David. 1998. *Writing Security: United States Foreign Policy and the Politics of Identity.* Minneapolis: Univ Of Minnesota Press.

Castro Varela, María do Mar, and Nikita Dhawan. 2015. *Postkoloniale Theorie: Eine kritische Einführung.* 2nd ed. Bielefeld: transcript.

Castro Varela, María do Mar and Alisha M.B. Heinemann. 2017. "'Eine Ziege für Afrika!' Globales Lernen unter postkolonialer Perspektive." In *Mit Bildung die Welt verändern? Globales Lernen für eine nachhaltige Entwicklung*, eds. Oliver Emde, Uwe Jakubczyk, Bernd Kappes, and Bernd Overwien, 38-54. Opladen, Berlin, Toronto: Verlag Barbara Budrich.

Chakrabarty, Dipesh. 2010. *Europa als Provinz: Perspektiven post-kolonialer Geschichtsschreibung*. Translated by Robin Cackett. Frankfurt am Main, New York: Campus Verlag.

Conrad, Sebastian. 2013. *Globalgeschichte: Eine Einführung*. München: C.H. Beck.

Conrad, Sebastian and Shalini Randeria. 2013. "Einleitung: Geteilte Geschichten – Europa in der postkolonialen Welt." In *Jenseits des Eurozentrismus: postkoloniale Perspektiven in den Geschichts- und Kulturwissenschaften*, eds. Sebastian Conrad, Shalini Randeria, and Regina Römhild, 2nd ed., 32-72. Frankfurt am Main, New York: Campus Verlag.

Döring, Jörg and Tristan Thielmann, eds. 2009. "Einleitung: Was lesen wir im Raum? Der Spatial Turn und das geheime Wissen der Geographen." In *Spatial Turn: Das Raumparadigma in den Kultur- und Sozialwissenschaften*, 2nd ed., 7-45. Bielefeld: Transcript.

Fenske, Uta, Daniel Groth, Klaus-Michael Guse, and Bärbel Kuhn, eds. 2015. *Kolonialismus und Dekolonisation in nationalen Geschichtskulturen und Erinnerungspolitiken in Europa. Module für den Geschichtsunterricht*. Frankfurt am Main: Lang

Frey, Barbara. 2019. *Respekt, Ehre, Verdienst? Die Upmanns: Geschichte eines globalen Familienunternehmens*. Unterrichtsmaterialienreihe Wissen um Globale Verflechtungen, 7. Bielefeld: kipu-Verlag.

Gärtner, Teresa. 2012. "Lesen Lernen: Über Die Bedeutung Historiografischer Medien für eine kritische Geschichtsschreibung jenseits von Texten." *WerkstattGeschichte* 61: 28-36.

Grewe, Bernd-Stefan. 2016. "Entgrenzte Räume und die Verortung des Globalen. Probleme und Potenziale für das historische Lernen." In *Geschichte im interdisziplinären Diskurs: Grenzziehungen – Grenzüberschreitungen – Grenzverschiebungen*, eds. Michael Sauer, Charlotte Bühl-Gramer, Anke John, Astrid Schwabe, Alfons Kenkmann, and Christian Kuchler, 297-320.

Beihefte zur Zeitschrift für Geschichtsdidaktik, 12. Göttingen: V & R Unipress.

Hall, Stuart. 2017. *Rassismus und kulturelle Identität.* 7th ed. Stuart Hall, Ausgewählte Schriften, 2. Hamburg: Argument Verlag.

Junge, Barbara. 2014. *Regulierung durch Evaluation in der Hochschulbildung: Zur Übersetzung internationaler Qualitätsstandards in Chile und Südafrika.* Baden-Baden: Nomos.

Kaltmeier, Olaf. 2012. *Politische Räume jenseits von Staat und Nation.* Das Politische als Kommunikation, 7. Göttingen: Wallstein Verlag.

———. 2014. "Inter-American Perspectives for the Rethinking of Area Studies." *Forum for Inter-American Research* 7 (3): 171-182.

———. 2019. "General Introduction to the Routledge Handbook to the History and Society of the Americas." In *The Routledge Handbook to the History and Society of the Americas*, eds. Olaf Kaltmeier, Josef Raab, Michael Stewart Foley, Alice Nash, Stefan Rinke, and Mario Rufer, 1-12. Abingdon, Oxon, NY: Routledge.

Kaltmeier, Olaf and Sarah Corona Berkin, eds. 2012. *Methoden dekolonialisieren: Eine Werkzeugkiste zur Demokratisierung der Sozial- und Kulturwissenschaften.* Münster: Westfälisches Dampfboot.

Kaltmeier, Olaf, Michael Stewart Foley, and Mario Rufer. 2019. "History and Society in the Americas in the 20th and 21st Centuries: Inter-American Thresholds and Critical Key Concepts." In *The Routledge Handbook to the History and Society of the Americas*, eds. Olaf Kaltmeier, Josef Raab, Michael Stewart Foley, Alice Nash, Stefan Rinke, and Mario Rufer, 207-221. Abingdon, Oxon, NY: Routledge.

KMK, BMZ, and EG, eds. 2016. *Curriculum Framework: Education for Sustainable Development.* 2nd updated and extended ed.

https://www.globaleslernen.de/sites/default/files/files/link-elements/curriculum_framework_education_for_sustainable_development_barrierefrei.pdf.

Koselleck, Reinhart. 2013 [2000]. *Zeitschichten: Studien zur Historik.* 3rd ed. Frankfurt am Main: Suhrkamp.

Lefebvre, Henri. 2000 [1974]. *La production de l'espace.* 4th ed. Ethnosociologie. Paris: Éd. Anthropos.

Lessenich, Stephan. 2016. *Neben uns die Sintflut: Die Externalisierungsgesellschaft und ihr Preis.* München: Hanser Berlin.

Lossau, Julia. 2012. "Spatial Turn." In *Handbuch Stadtsoziologie,* ed. Frank Eckardt, 185-198. Wiesbaden: Springer VS.

Middell, Matthias. 2009. "Der Spatial Turn und das Interesse an der Globalisierung in der Geschichtswissenschaft." In *Spatial Turn: das Raumparadigma in den Kultur- und Sozialwissenschaften,* eds. Jörg Döring and Tristan Thielmann, 2nd ed., 103-123. Bielefeld: Transcript.

Mies, Maria. 2015. *Patriarchat und Kapital.* Updated and extended ed. München: bge-verlag.

Mignolo, Walter. 2000. *Local Histories/Global Designs: Coloniality, Subaltern Knowledges, and Border Thinking.* Princeton Studies in Culture/Power/History. Princeton, NJ: Princeton University Press.

———. 2012. *Epistemischer Ungehorsam: Rhetorik der Moderne, Logik der Kolonialität und Grammatik der Dekolonialität.* Eds. Jens Kastner and Tom Waibel. Wien, Berlin: Verlag Turia+ Kant.

Ministerium für Schule und Weiterbildung NRW, ed. 2014. "Kernlehrplan Für Die Sek II Gymnasium/Gesamtschule in Nordrhein-Westfalen. Geschichte." https://www.schulentwicklung. nrw.de/lehrplaene/upload/klp_SII/ge/KLP_GOSt_Geschichte.pdf.

Moulian, Tomás. 1997. *Chile Actual: Anatomía de un mito*. Colección Sin Norte. Santiago, Chile: ARCIS Universidad / LOM Ediciones.

Müller-Matthis, Stefan and Alexander Wohnig, eds. 2017. "Konstruktionen der ungleichen Partizipation in Schulbüchern. Zur Einführung." In *Wie Schulbücher Rollen formen: Konstruktionen der ungleichen Partizipation in Schulbüchern*, 5-11. Schwalbach/Ts: Wochenschau Wissenschaft.

Neues Deutschand. 1993. "St. Petersburger Politiker will Diktatur. Pinochet als Vorbild." *Online-Archiv Neues Deutschland* (31 December 1993).

Ngozi Adichie, Chimamanda. 2009. "The Danger of a Single Story." *TED Talk*. https://www.youtube.com/watch?v=D9Ihs241zeg.

Osterhammel, Jürgen. 1998. "*Die Wiederkehr des Raumes: Geopolitik, Geohistorie und Historische Geographie*." *Neue Politische Literatur* 43: 374-396.

Oswalt, Vadim. 2010. "Das Wo zum Was und Wann. Der 'Spatial Turn' und seine Bedeutung für die Geschichtsdidaktik." *Geschichte in Wissenschaft und Unterricht* 61, 4: 220-233.

———. 2016. *Planung von Unterrichtseinheiten: Wie man Geschichte (an)ordnen kann*. Kleine Reihe Geschichte, Didaktik und Methodik. Schwalbach/Ts: Wochenschau Verlag.

———. 2019. *Karten als Quelle und Darstellung: Historische Karten und Geschichtskarten im Unterricht*. Forum Historisches Lernen. Frankfurt am Main: Wochenschau Verlag.

Petersen, Mirko. 2018. *Kalter Krieg in Lateinamerika: Unterrichtsbausteine für den Geschichtsunterricht in der Sekundarstufe II*. Nicole Schwabe ed. Unterrichtsmaterialienreihe Wissen um globale Verflechtungen, 5. Bielefeld: kipu-Verlag.

Pike, Graham and David Selby (1999): *In the Global Classroom, Vol. I + II*. Toronto: Pippin Publishing.

Popp, Susanne. 2005. "Antworten auf neue Herausforderungen. Welt- und globalgeschichtliche Perspektivierung des Historischen Lernens." *Geschichte in Wissenschaft und Unterricht* 56, 9: 491-507.

Popp, Susanne and Johanna Forster, eds. 2008. *Curriculum Weltgeschichte: Interdisziplinäre Zugänge zu einem global orientierten Geschichtsunterricht.* Forum Historisches Lernen. Schwalbach/Ts: Wochenschau-Verl.

Quijano, Aníbal. 2016. *Kolonialität der Macht, Eurozentrismus und Lateinamerika.* Wien, Berlin: Turia+Kant.

Randeria, Shalini and Regina Römhild. 2013. "Das postkoloniale: Einleitung." In *Jenseits des Eurozentrismus: Postkoloniale Perspektiven in den Geschichts- und Kulturwissenschaften*, eds. Sebastian Conrad, Shalini Randeria, and Regina Römhild, 2nd ed., 9-31. Frankfurt am Main, New York: Campus Verlag.

Riekenberg, Michael and Georg-Eckert-Institut für Internationale Schulbuchforschung, eds. 1990. *Lateinamerika: Geschichtsunterricht, Geschichtslehrbücher, Geschichtsbewusstsein.* Studien zur Internationalen Schulbuchforschung, 66. Frankfurt am Main: M. Diesterweg.

Said, Edward W. 2010 [1978]. *Orientalismus.* Translated by Hans Günter Holl. 2nd ed. Frankfurt am Main: S. Fischer.

Sauer, Michael. 2012. *Geschichte unterrichten: Eine Einführung in die Didaktik und Methodik.* 10th updated and extended ed. Seelze: Klett/Kallmeyer.

Schlögel, Karl. 2016 [2003]. *Im Raume lesen wir die Zeit: Über Zivilisationsgeschichte und Geopolitik.* 5th ed. Frankfurt am Main: Fischer.

Schmeinck, Daniela. 2007. *Wie Kinder die Welt sehen: eine empirische Ländervergleichsstudie zur räumlichen Vorstellung von Grundschulkindern.* Klinkhard-Forschung. Bad Heilbrunn: Klinkhardt.

Schwabe, Nicole. 2017. "La Educación de Pinochet." In Kaltmeier, Olaf and Nicole Schwabe, eds. 2017. *¿Cachai Chile? Sociedad. Memoria. Conflictos Actuales: Unterrichtsbausteine für den Spanischunterricht.* Unterrichtsmaterialienreihe Wissen um Globale Verflechtungen, 4, 35-47 Bielefeld: kipu.

Schwabe, Nicole, Jochen Kemner, Anner Tittor, and Olaf Kaltmeier. 2018. *CIAS Concept Dossier. Entrelazamientos interamericanos en la enseñanza. Reflexiones conceptuales sobre la serie de materiales escolares ›Aprendiendo sobre entrelazamientos globales‹,* kipu Online Publication, URL: www.uni-bielefeld.de/cias/unterrichtsmaterialien.

Soja, Edward. 2003. "Thirdspace. Die Erweiterung des geographischen Blicks." In *Kulturgeographie: Aktuelle Ansätze und Entwicklungen*, eds. Hans Gebhardt, Paul Reuber, and Günther Wolkersdorfer, 269-288. Heidelberg: Spektrum, Akad.-Verl.

———. 2008. "Vom 'Zeitgeist' zum 'Raumgeist'. New Twists on the Spatial Turn." In *Spatial Turn: Das Raumparadigma in den Kultur- und Sozialwissenschaften*, eds. Jörg Döring and Tristan Thielmann, 2nd ed., 241-262. Bielefeld: Transcript.

Thiery, Peter. 2007. "Lateinamerika: Politische Transformation Zur Demokratie." In *BpB-Dossier: Lateinamerika*, ed. BpB. http://www.bpb.de/internationales/amerika/lateinamerika/44598/transformation?p=0#bio0.

Universidad de Buenos Aires. 2009. *Orientaciones para el estudio de la bibliografía obligatoria: Sociología.* Buenos Aires: Eudeba.

Völkel, Bärbel. 2013. "Von ungewollten Nebenwirkungen eines traditionellen chronologischen Geschichtsunterrichts." *Historische Mitteilungen* 26: 401-412.

———. 2016. "Nationalismus – Ethizismus – Rassismus?" In *Historisches Lernen als Rassismuskritik*, eds. Christina Isabel Brüning, Lars Deile, and Matin Lücke, 49-70. Forum Historisches Lernen. Schwalbach: Wochenschau Verlag.

Wagner-Kyora, Georg, Jens Wilczek, and Friedrich Huneke, eds. 2008. *Transkulturelle Geschichtsdidaktik: Kompetenzen und Unterrichtskonzepte. Studien zur Weltgeschichte.* Schwalbach/ Ts: Wochenschau-Verl.

Weber, Wolfgang E. J. 2019. "Die Umbrüche des Jahres 1989 globalgeschichtlich betrachtet – Perspektiven für den Geschichtsunterricht." Konferenzbericht. Universität Augsburg: AK Internationales der Konferenz für Geschichtsdidaktik. https://www. philhist.uni-augsburg.de/lehrstuehle/geschichte/didaktik/intern/ downloads_internal/ac_world_history_conference_report-2019. pdf.

Welthaus Bielefeld, ed. 2013. *Textilien – Weltreise einer Jeans. Bildungseinheit für das Fach Gesellschaftslehre.* Bielefeld. https:// www.welthaus.de/fileadmin/user_upload/Bildung/Unterrichts materialien_Reise_einer_Jeans.pdf.

Wenzlhuemer, Roland. 2017. *Globalgeschichte schreiben: Eine Einführung in 6 Episoden.* Konstanz: UVK Verlagsgesellschaft mbH.

INTER-AMERICAN STUDIES
Cultures – Societies – History

ESTUDIOS INTERAMERICANOS
Culturas – Sociedades – Historia

This interdisciplinary series examines national and transnational issues in the cultures, societies, and histories of the Americas. It creates a forum for a critical academic dialogue between North and South, promoting an inter-American paradigm that shifts the scholarly focus from methodological nationalism to the wider context of the Western Hemisphere.

Vol. 1
Raab, Josef, Sebastian Thies, and Daniela Noll-Opitz, eds. *Screening the Americas: Narration of Nation in Documentary Film / Proyectando las Américas: Narración de la nación en el cine documental.* 2011. 472 pp.

WVT Wissenschaftlicher Verlag Trier	ISBN 978-3-86821-331-7	€ 29,50
Bilingual Press / Editorial Bilingüe	ISBN 978-1-931010-83-2	$ 29.50

Vol. 2
Raussert, Wilfried, and Michelle Habell-Pallán, eds. *Cornbread and Cuchifritos: Ethnic Identity Politics, Transnationalization, and Transculturation in American Urban Popular Music.* 2011. 292 pp.

WVT Wissenschaftlicher Verlag Trier	ISBN 978-3-86821-265-5	€ 29,50
Bilingual Press / Editorial Bilingüe	ISBN 978- 1-931010-80-1	$ 29.50

Vol. 3
Butler, Martin, Jens Martin Gurr, and Olaf Kaltmeier, eds. *EthniCities: Metropolitan Cultures and Ethnic Identities in the Americas.* 2011. 268 pp.

WVT Wissenschaftlicher Verlag Trier	ISBN 978-3-86821-310-2	€ 29,50
Bilingual Press / Editorial Bilingüe	ISBN 978-1-931010-81-8	$ 29.50

Vol. 4
Gurr, Jens Martin, and Wilfried Raussert, eds. *Cityscapes in the Americas and Beyond: Representations of Urban Complexity in Literature and Film.* 2011. 300 pp.

WVT Wissenschaftlicher Verlag Trier	ISBN 978-3-86821-324-9	€ 29,50
Bilingual Press / Editorial Bilingüe	ISBN 978-1-931010-82-5	$ 29.50

Vol. 5

Kirschner, Luz Angélica, ed. *Expanding* Latinidad*: An Inter-American Perspective.* 2012. 292 pp.

WVT Wissenschaftlicher Verlag Trier   ISBN 978-3-86821-309-6   € 29,50
Bilingual Press / Editorial Bilingüe   ISBN 978-1-931010-84-9 $ 29.50

Vol. 6

Raussert, Wilfried, and Graciela Martínez-Zalce, eds. *(Re)Discovering 'America': Road Movies and Other Travel Narratives in North America / (Re)Descubriendo 'América': Road movie y otras narrativas de viaje en América del Norte.* 2012. 252 pp.

WVT Wissenschaftlicher Verlag Trier   ISBN 978-3-86821-384-3   € 29,50
Bilingual Press / Editorial Bilingüe   ISBN 978-1-931010-91-7 $ 29.50

Vol. 7

Kaltmeier, Olaf, ed. *Transnational Americas: Envisioning Inter-American Area Studies in Globalization Processes.* 2013. 278 pp.

WVT Wissenschaftlicher Verlag Trier   ISBN 978-3-86821-415-4   € 29,50
Bilingual Press / Editorial Bilingüe   ISBN 978-1-931010-92-4 $ 29.50

Vol. 8

Raab, Josef, and Alexander Greiffenstern, eds. *Interculturalism in North America: Canada, the United States, Mexico, and Beyond.* 2013. 312 pp.

WVT Wissenschaftlicher Verlag Trier   ISBN 978-3-86821-460-4   € 29,50
Bilingual Press / Editorial Bilingüe   ISBN 978-1-931010-99-3 $ 29.50

Vol. 9

Raab, Josef, ed. *New World Colors: Ethnicity, Belonging, and Difference in the Americas.* 2014. 418 pp.

WVT Wissenschaftlicher Verlag Trier   ISBN 978-3-86821-461-1   € 29,50
Bilingual Press / Editorial Bilingüe   ISBN 978-1-939743-00-8 $ 39.50

Vol. 10

Roth, Julia. *Occidental Readings, Decolonial Practices: A Selection on Gender, Genre, and Coloniality in the Americas.* 2014. 284 pp.

WVT Wissenschaftlicher Verlag Trier   ISBN 978-3-86821-446-8   € 26,50
Bilingual Press / Editorial Bilingüe   ISBN 978-1-939743-07-7 $ 32.50

Vol. 11

Thies, Sebastian, Gabriele Pisarz-Ramirez, and Luzelena Gutiérrez de Velasco, eds. *Of Fatherlands and Motherlands: Gender and Nation in the Americas / De Patrias y Matrias: Género y nación en las Américas.* 2015. 344 pp.

WVT Wissenschaftlicher Verlag Trier   ISBN 978-3-86821-528-1   € 29,50
Bilingual Press / Editorial Bilingüe   ISBN 978-1-939743-08-4 $ 39.50

Vol. 12

Fuchs, Rebecca. *Caribbeanness as a Global Phenomenon: Junot Díaz, Edwidge Danticat, and Cristina García*. 2014. 298 pp.

| WVT Wissenschaftlicher Verlag Trier | ISBN 978-3-86821-533-5 | € 26,50 |
| Bilingual Press / Editorial Bilingüe | ISBN 978-1-939743-09-1 | $ 32.50 |

Vol. 13

Andres, Julia. *¡Cuéntame algo! – Chicana Narrative Beyond the Borderlands*. 2015. 202 pp.

| WVT Wissenschaftlicher Verlag Trier | ISBN 978-3-86821-569-4 | € 25,00 |
| Bilingual Press / Editorial Bilingüe | ISBN 978-1-939743-11-4 | $ 28.50 |

Vol. 14

Hertlein, Saskia. *Tales of Transformation: Emerging Adulthood, Migration, and Ethnicity in Contemporary American Literature*. 2014. 228 pp.

| WVT Wissenschaftlicher Verlag Trier | ISBN 978-3-86821-570-0 | € 25,00 |
| Bilingual Press / Editorial Bilingüe | ISBN 978-1-939743-10-7 | $ 31.50 |

Vol. 15

Raab, Josef, and Saskia Hertlein, eds. *Spaces – Communities – Discourses: Charting Identity and Belonging in the Americas*. 2016. 382 pp.

| WVT Wissenschaftlicher Verlag Trier | ISBN 978-3-86821-590-8 | € 29,50 |
| Bilingual Press / Editorial Bilingüe | ISBN 978-1-939743-13-8 | $ 39.50 |

Vol. 16

Mehring, Frank, ed. *The Mexico Diary: Winold Reiss between Vogue Mexico and Harlem Renaissance. An Illustrated Trilingual Edition with Commentary and Musical Interpretation* (includes color plates and audio CD). 2016. 244 pp.

| WVT Wissenschaftlicher Verlag Trier | ISBN 978-3-86821-594-6 | € 29,50 |
| Bilingual Press / Editorial Bilingüe | ISBN 978-1-939743-14-5 | $ 39.50 |

Vol. 17

Raussert, Wilfried, Brian Rozema, Yolanda Campos, and Marius Littschwager, eds. *Key Tropes in Inter-American Studies: Perspectives from the* forum for inter-american research (fiar). 2015. 374 pp.

| WVT Wissenschaftlicher Verlag Trier | ISBN 978-3-86821-627-1 | € 29,50 |
| Bilingual Press / Editorial Bilingüe | ISBN 978-1-939743-16-9 | $ 39.50 |

Vol. 19

Rehm, Lukas, Jochen Kemner, and Olaf Kaltmeier, eds. *Politics of Entanglement in the Americas: Connecting Transnational Flows and Local Perspectives*. 2017. 226 pp.

| WVT Wissenschaftlicher Verlag Trier | ISBN 978-3-86821-675-2 | € 27,50 |
| Bilingual Press / Editorial Bilingüe | ISBN 978 1 939743 17 6 | $ 32.50 |

Vol. 20

Britt Arredondo, Christopher. *Imperial Idiocy: A Reflection on Forced Displacement in the Americas.* 2017. 194 pp.

| WVT Wissenschaftlicher Verlag Trier | ISBN 978-3-86821-706-3 | € 26,50 |
| Bilingual Press / Editorial Bilingüe | ISBN 978-1-939743-20-6 | $ 30.00 |

Vol. 21

Schemien, Alexia. *Of Virgins, Curanderas, and Wrestler Saints: Un/Doing Religion in Contemporary Mexican American Literature.* 2018. 218 pp.

| WVT Wissenschaftlicher Verlag Trier | ISBN 978-3-86821-724-7 | € 27,50 |
| Bilingual Press / Editorial Bilingüe | ISBN 978-1-939743-22-0 | $ 32.50 |

Vol. 22

Fulger, Maria Diana. *The Cuban Post-Socialist Exotic: Contemporary U.S. American Travel Narratives about Cuba.* 2020. 266 pp.

| WVT Wissenschaftlicher Verlag Trier | ISBN 978-3-86821-769-8 | € 32,50 |
| Bilingual Press / Editorial Bilingüe | ISBN 978-1-939743-27-5 | $ 36.00 |

Vol. 24

Kaltmeier, Olaf, Mirko Petersen, Wilfried Raussert, and Julia Roth, eds. *Cherishing the Past, Envisioning the Future. Entangled Practises of Heritage and Utopia in the Americas.* 2021. 176 pp.

| WVT Wissenschaftlicher Verlag Trier | ISBN 978-3-86821-804-6 | € 23,50 |
| UNO University of New Orleans Press | ISBN 978-1-60801-206-0 | $ 27.50 |

Vol. 26

Raussert, Wilfried. *'What's Going On': How Music Shapes the Social.* 2021. 224 pp.

| WVT Wissenschaftlicher Verlag Trier | ISBN 978-3-86821-811-4 | € 28,50 |
| UNO University of New Orleans Press | ISBN 978-1-60801-199-5 | $ 34.00 |

Vol. 27

Frank-Job, Barbara. *Immigration as a Process: Temporality Concepts in Blogs of Latin American Immigrants to Québec.* 2021. 138 pp.

| WVT Wissenschaftlicher Verlag Trier | ISBN 978-3-86821-820-6 | € 20,00 |
| UNO University of New Orleans Press | ISBN 978-1-60801-215-2 | $ 24.00 |

Vol. 28

Roth, Julia. *Can Feminism Trump Populism? Right-Wing Trends and Intersectional Contestations in the Americas.* 2021. 168 pp.

| WVT Wissenschaftlicher Verlag Trier | ISBN 978-3-86821-821-3 | € 23,00 |
| UNO University of New Orleans Press | ISBN 978-1-60801-205-3 | $ 26.00 |

Vol. 30

Buitrago Valencia, Clara. *Missionaries: Migrants or Expatriates? Guatemalan Pentecostal Leaders in Los Angeles.* 2021. 236 pp.

| WVT Wissenschaftlicher Verlag Trier | ISBN 978-3-86821-818-3 | € 28,50 |
| UNO University of New Orleans Press | ISBN 978-1-60801-210-7 | $ 34.50 |

Vol. 31

Schwabe, Nicole. *De-Centering History Education: Creating Knowledge of Global Entanglements.* 2021. 92 pp.

| WVT Wissenschaftlicher Verlag Trier | ISBN 978-3-86821-828-2 | € 18,00 |
| UNO University of New Orleans Press | ISBN 978-1-60801-214-5 | $ 21.00 |

Vol. 32

Manke, Albert. *Coping with Discrimination and Exclusion. Experiences of Free Chinese Migrants in the Americas in a Transregional and Diachronic Perspective.* 2021. 162 pp.

| WVT Wissenschaftlicher Verlag Trier | ISBN 978-3-86821-829-9 | € 23,00 |
| UNO University of New Orleans Press | ISBN 978-1-60801-207-7 | $ 27.00 |

Vol. 33

Rohland, Eleonora. *Entangled Histories and the Environment? Socio-Environmental Transformations in the Caribbean, 1492-1800.* 2021. 92 pp.

| WVT Wissenschaftlicher Verlag Trier | ISBN 978-3-86821-833-6 | € 18,00 |
| UNO University of New Orleans Press | ISBN 978-1-60801-208-4 | $ 21.00 |

Vol. 34

Kaltmeier, Olaf. *National Parks from North to South. An Entangled History of Conservation and Colonization in Argentina.* 2021. 208 pp.

| WVT Wissenschaftlicher Verlag Trier | ISBN 978-3-86821-834-3 | € 27,50 |
| UNO University of New Orleans Press | ISBN 978-1-60801-204-6 | $ 32.50 |

Vol. 35

Raussert, Wilfried. *Off the Grid. Art Practices and Public Space.* 2021. 232 pp.

| WVT Wissenschaftlicher Verlag Trier | ISBN 978-3-86821-835-0 | € 29,50 |
| UNO University of New Orleans Press | ISBN 978-1-60801-213-8 | $ 34.50 |

Vol. 36

Ravasio, Paola. *This Train Is Not Bound to Glory. A Study of Literary Trainscapes.* 2021. 114 pp.

| WVT Wissenschaftlicher Verlag Trier | ISBN 978-3-86821-836-7 | € 18,00 |
| UNO University of New Orleans Press | ISBN 978-1-60801-216-9 | $ 21.00 |

Vol. 37
Schäfer, Heinrich Wilhelm. *Protestant 'Sects' and the Spirit of (Anti-)Imperialism. Religious Entanglements in the Americas.* 2021. 242 pp.

WVT Wissenschaftlicher Verlag Trier	ISBN 978-3-86821-855-9	€ 29,50
UNO University of New Orleans Press	ISBN 978-1-60801-209-1	$ 34.50